Survival and Separation on the River Kwai

The Ordeal of a Japanese Prisoner of War and His Family

Ian Roberts

Pen & Sword
MILITARY

First published in Great Britain in 2023 by
Pen & Sword Military
An imprint of
Pen & Sword Books Ltd
Yorkshire – Philadelphia

Copyright © Ian Roberts 2023

ISBN 978 1 39904 955 9

The right of Ian Roberts to be identified as Author of this work has been asserted by him in accordance with the Copyright, Designs and Patents Act 1988.

A CIP catalogue record for this book is
available from the British Library.

All rights reserved. No part of this book may be reproduced or transmitted in any form or by any means, electronic or mechanical including photocopying, recording or by any information storage and retrieval system, without permission from the Publisher in writing.

Typeset by Mac Style
Printed in the UK by CPI Group (UK) Ltd, Croydon, CR0 4YY.

Pen & Sword Books Limited incorporates the imprints of Atlas, Archaeology, Aviation, Discovery, Family History, Fiction, History, Maritime, Military, Military Classics, Politics, Select, Transport, True Crime, Air World, Frontline Publishing, Leo Cooper, Remember When, Seaforth Publishing, The Praetorian Press, Wharncliffe Local History, Wharncliffe Transport, Wharncliffe True Crime, White Owl and After the Battle.

For a complete list of Pen & Sword titles please contact

PEN & SWORD BOOKS LIMITED
47 Church Street, Barnsley, South Yorkshire, S70 2AS, England
E-mail: enquiries@pen-and-sword.co.uk
Website: www.pen-and-sword.co.uk

Or

PEN AND SWORD BOOKS
1950 Lawrence Rd, Havertown, PA 19083, USA
E-mail: Uspen-and-sword@casematepublishers.com
Website: www.penandswordbooks.com

Dedication

For Eunice, Eric and Lilian and for Sasha: please remember. With thanks to my wife and parents, the FEPOW Facebook Community and the Thailand Burma Railway Centre (TBRC).

Contents

Introduction		ix
Chapter 1	September 1941: Mobilization (Again)	1
Chapter 2	Observations on the Territorial Army	2
Chapter 3	October 1941: Movement from the UK to the Middle East	4
Chapter 4	Arrival at Halifax, Nova Scotia	6
Chapter 5	December 1941: Cape Town, South Africa	13
Chapter 6	1942: Bombay, India and Ahmednagar	20
Chapter 7	January 1942: Singapore	32
Chapter 8	Home Front: February–May 1942	41
Chapter 9	February–May 1942: Changi, Singapore	58
Chapter 10	Home Front: August–October 1942	61
Chapter 11	May–October 1942: River Valley Road Camp, Singapore	67
Chapter 12	Home Front: November 1942–May 1943	73
Chapter 13	October 1942–May 1943: Wampo, Thailand	78
Chapter 14	May–August 1943: Tonchan Main Camp and Tonchan Spring Camp, Thailand	88
Chapter 15	Home Front: May 1943–March 1944	94
Chapter 16	August 1943–March 1944: Kinsayo and Kinsayo North, Thailand	101

Chapter 17	Home Front: March 1944–June 1945	109
Chapter 18	March 1944–June 1945: Tamuan, Thailand	115
Chapter 19	June–August 1945: Pratchai, Thailand	125
Chapter 20	August–November 1945	135
Chapter 21	November 1945–1946: Return and Readjustment	146
Chapter 22	Epilogue	152

Appendix: Mrs Robinson's Account of PoW Life	156
Maps	165
Bibliography	169
Index	170

Introduction

Eric and Eunice were my paternal grandparents. Eunice died in 1980, before I was born, and Eric died in 2001. Eric told us very little of his military service. We knew he'd served with the British Expeditionary Force (BEF) in France and was captured at Singapore in 1942. He then spent three and a half years as a prisoner of war working on the railway adjacent to the River Kwai. Although we asked, his recollections from this time were clearly very painful so we didn't pursue them. Following Eric's death my father began clearing the house, during which process he found a typed manuscript of 'memoirs' and a bundle of letters. The notes covered Eric's military service and his memories of his immediate family. The letters were written by Eric and sent to Eunice during the war. Eric's close friend George White, who served with him and was his closest friend in the camps, reviewed the memoirs and provided notes, so they are 'verified'. There was also Eunice's scrapbook and diaries from the time that detail how the Fall of Singapore affected life on the home front. The combination of all these sources has provided the basis for this book.

It's worth summarizing the lives of Eric and Eunice as this provides the personal context for the story. Eric was born in July 1918 in Burton-on-Trent. His father, Frank Roberts, volunteered for military service in 1914 with the South Staffordshire Regiment. He returned home in 1919 a broken man, suffering from the effects of gas poisoning and 'trench fever'; he was almost certainly badly affected by post-traumatic stress disorder. The effects of his illness entitled him to the war invalid's badge and an additional pension. When Eric was less than 2 years old his family sent him to live elsewhere. Eric never understood why and no reason was ever given. Possibly the pressure of having a young child at home with a traumatized war veteran was too much. Eric never forgave his parents or his sister Barbara for pushing him out, and they also showed little interest in his wellbeing or development. When Eric was about 18 months old he was discovered in a poor state of health and was taken in by Lilian Degg (his mother's sister) and her husband James (Uncle Jim) who brought him up alongside their own son, Ronald. Eric continued to suffer from ill health as a child and at the age of 12 he spent a month in hospital recovering from rheumatic fever. He was informed by his doctor that 'if he took life quietly he might live a reasonable length of time.' He was also instructed to take no part in sport or games.

Eric was active in the Young Men's Christian Association (YMCA) and met Eunice Lowe on one of their trips away in 1938. Eunice was born in 1917 in Atherstone in Warwickshire. She was the daughter of the second wife of John H. Lowe and was the youngest of six siblings: two brothers, one sister and two half-brothers and one half-sister. John was a wealthy farmer and Eunice was educated privately. Despite their very different backgrounds, Eric and Eunice had much in common: their faith, interest in the natural world and a unique sense of humour.

In 1938 another war with Germany appeared likely and in May 1939 the Militia Act reintroduced conscription. The generation whose fathers had served in the First World War, and some who had been brought up by widows, were being called up. Eric could have avoided conscription as he was on a commercial training course at the time; however, he felt that 'a year' of military service would do him good. Consequently, he was one of the first men to be called up and he reported to the Regimental Depot of the Sherwood Foresters at Normanton Barracks in Derby on 15 June 1939. They were to serve with the 1st Battalion of the Sherwood Foresters (Regular Army), issued with the new battledress and, in Eric's case, a much-used .303 Lee-Enfield rifle. Eric wrote that basic training included weapon instruction on the .303 rifle, .303 Bren Light Machine Gun, .505 Boys Anti-Tank Rifle, No. 38 Mills Grenade and also some were trained on the 2in mortar. There was a very good gym with Regular Army instructors and they had practice in judging distance and also in assessing land for giving and receiving firing instructions. After several months eighteen men were selected for signal training and Eric was one of these. In November 1939, these men were then posted to the 1/5th Battalion Sherwood Foresters, a Territorial Army (TA) regiment, then at Aldershot.

On the outbreak of war the militia units were absorbed into the TA. The original militia men were serving as full-time soldiers and were used to the discipline of the Regular Army. The territorial units comprised volunteers recruited before war was declared and who served during weekends and some weekday nights. It was a very closed community and there was considerable animosity between some TA members and the men from militia units. The 1/5 Foresters was made up of an HQ Company and four rifle companies: A, B, C and D Companies, the battalion being 1,000 men in total. As the 1/5 Foresters was a TA unit, many of its ranks and officers were local men from around Derbyshire.

It was commanded by the charismatic Lieutenant Colonel Harold Hutchinson Lilly, a local man from Spondon, Derbyshire. Lieutenant Colonel Lilly was commissioned into the battalion in 1915 and served with the 1/5 Foresters on the Western Front during the First World War. In July 1916 he led his platoon into an attack at Gomel, he reached the German trenches and took a number of prisoners. However, the attack was unsupported and the captors became captives. He spent the next two years as a prisoner of war (PoW). He never married and was devoted to the regiment. His resilience, strength of character and previous experience of captivity ensured that the morale of the regiment remained high and as a result he was awarded the Order of the British Empire (OBE) for his services in the PoW camps in the Far East. He was also the inspiration for Colonel Nicholson in the 1957 David Lean film *The Bridge on the River Kwai*, a poor epitaph. Lieutenant Colonel Lilly used his previous PoW experience to extract concessions from the Japanese. He fought extremely hard for his men at considerable personal risk and saved many, many lives. He survived the war, but his health was broken and he died at home in Spondon in 1954 aged 60.

In late November 1939 the 1/5 Foresters sailed from Southampton to France to join the second line of the BEF in Brittany. The Foresters joined the 25th Independent Division as 'lines of communications' troops which involved guarding railways, petrol and ammunition dumps, in their case around Blain. While in France, Eric became fairly fluent in French and was put forward for work with the Intelligence Corps by one of the officers. However, the Company Commanding Officer (Major F.W. Barnett) was away at the time and upon his return the order was cancelled. Eric was 'too useful' and became the company clerk instead.

One company (A Company) of the Foresters found themselves attached to the 51st Highland Division who provided the rearguard for the retreating troops at Dunkirk. They were mostly captured in 1940.

Without any means of defending themselves against German tanks, the remaining men of HQ, B, C and D Companies (including Eric) retreated from the advancing German armoured units. Eventually they embarked at Cherbourg; however, more men of the Foresters were lost when HMS *Lancastria* was bombed and sunk. The remaining troops returned to Southampton on 14 June 1940 (five weeks after Dunkirk). During the next few months the men who had been lost in France were replaced and many of these new recruits came from the south-east, including London.

Eric was always disappointed that his service in France was never recognized. Albeit in a second-line role, he was proud to have been with the first British troops to take part in the Second World War. In the First World War, those who served in 1914 were awarded the 1914 Star, which came with a clasp for service between August and November. Eric believed that there would be something similar for the Second World War, but no official insignia was ever awarded.

The 1/5 Foresters had returned home; however, until 1941 the outlook was particularly bleak. Europe was dominated by Nazi and Fascist regimes, and free Europe had fallen. The USA was formally 'neutral' until December 1941, and the Soviet Union had signed a non-aggression pact with Nazi Germany and would not enter the war until June 1941. Therefore, the focus for Britain was on the imminent Nazi invasion, so from mid-1940 to September 1941 the 1/5 Foresters were on home defence duties.

As the war in mainland Europe appeared to be over, the struggle continued in Africa and the Far East by British Imperial forces. The 1/5 Foresters were sent to Scotland in winter 1940 for training, then becoming part of the 18th Division. They were mobilized again in September 1941, which is when we join Eric's story.

Chapter 1

September 1941: Mobilization (Again)

In about September 1941, we found ourselves mobilizing once again for service overseas. The Battalion was built up to strength of 1001 Officers and Other Ranks (ORs). Some men were posted elsewhere and others joined. About this time, 'Radio Location' was heard mentioned for the first time. This was to be known later as 'Radar'. Men were required for training in this and two or three of our men left the Battalion for this. I met two of these men after the war and found that they had had an interesting time in Europe maintaining equipment for both British and American forces.

Men were issued with tropical kit and we now found ourselves with full marching order and two kit bags (one white and one blue). There is a lot of work involved in moving a Battalion overseas and much of the administrative work fell to me. I worked long hours, very often on my own. Apart from Army matters, I found myself dealing with some private affairs, things like correspondence in arranging Powers of Attorney.

As a little aside, the Adjutant complained about bad language in the Battalion Orderly Room and insisted we should have a 'swear box' into which we placed 1d when we swore. This didn't worry me unduly, it was the Adjutant who was usually the guilty party. After some weeks when the box was quite heavy, I discovered it was missing. Enquiries eventually led me to the Adjutant who said 'Yes, I've had the b...., it was my money anyway' – just another indication of his character.

The adjutant was Arthur William Coxon (P/124325), who would later become a captain. He was a married Derby man and returned home in 1945 (Housley, 1995).

Chapter 2

Observations on the Territorial Army

Having served in the militia as a full-time soldier, subject to Regular Army discipline for five months and then in a TA unit from November 1939, Eric was able to compare the culture and approach of the two organizations:

> I was called up in the knowledge that I would be in the Army full time twenty-four hours a day. Before serving with the 1/5, the Officers and Non-Commissioned Officers (NCOs) I had dealings with were all fairly long-serving Regular Army soldiers. They were accustomed to maintaining discipline over men who were under a fixed contract of service. Also, the Officers and NCOs had the backing of enforceable regulations and the weight of military law. Apart from where civil offences were concerned, the Army administered its own law. So in the first five months of my service I fitted into this pattern and accepted it. Conversely, members of the TA were part-time soldiers who in peacetime could not be subjected to the same discipline as if they were in the Regular Army.
>
> Unlike a conscript army which came from all walks of life, the TA came from a fairly narrow band. Officers may at some time have emerged from College or Grammar School Officer Training Corps, whereas the ORs were in the main manual workers from various trades. There were few administrative types. TA members appearing only at weekends, possibly some week-day nights and for a two-week annual camp, could hardly be described as a well-disciplined force. The NCOs were drawn from this intake and many could not be said to be foreman material. I believe that many had been promoted to fill a place in an establishment and it was to be proved that many were not anxious to accept the responsibilities accorded to their rank. Sadly, there was general sloppiness.

In the case of my own battalion, over half the strength were reservists or conscripts and not TA. However, the bulk of the Commissioned Officers were from the TA. With TA officers, the tendency was that, where promotion was concerned, TA men known to them were promoted and they were not necessarily the best. It took a long time before conscripts appeared as Warrant Officers (WOs) and NCOs. In the peacetime TA, there was an element of Regular Army soldiers. I think there was a Regular Adjutant, a Quartermaster and a number of Permanent Staff Instructors, possibly a Regimental Sergeant Major. However, these men did not have the backing they would have had in the Regular Army. Part-timers could not be disciplined in the same way. However, there were some very fine, brave men of TA origin who would have shown up very differently when war came, had they been under different circumstances.

Chapter 3

October 1941: Movement from the UK to the Middle East

In October 1941, mobilization of the Battalion was complete. I arranged for someone to take my bicycle to Burton-on-Trent. Our transport, Bren Carriers etc. had left by other means and eventually the 1001 Officers and ORs were to leave from Penkridge Railway Station for Liverpool. There were two trains; on the first were loaded 501 men. The remaining 500 men were marched to the station from the Hall and I was given the job to remain until the end but to leave in a truck and arrive at the station before the men. I duly did this and was standing at the top of the steps leading to the platform when the first man arrived. The train was waiting and I counted 499 on and with myself 500. Away to Liverpool, alongside the docks there and immediately aboard a ship; the P&O vessel SS *Orcades*. Being a Sergeant when I got aboard I was handed a boarding card which allocated me a bunk on C Deck. I shared this cabin with five others of similar rank. I later discovered that although I was comfortably accommodated, the men generally were accommodated on mess decks. These were fairly large areas between decks where a series of tables had been fixed to the deck and where men had their meals and spent a fair amount of time. At night, hammocks were slung over the tables in which the men slept. In the daytime, hammocks were stowed in the bulkheads. The circumstances were not of the best.

Within a couple of days or so men had got their sea legs and had settled down to shipboard routine. The ship we were on had recently been in at the Cape (South Africa) and our food was good. There was also a ship's canteen which was well stocked. There were several troop ships in the convoy, the escort being a cruiser and two destroyers. There was a plane lashed to the deck of the cruiser which was launched by a catapult. It seemed that in the event of it being launched, the pilot could not land on the ship; he was required to

October 1941: Movement from the UK to the Middle East

ditch in the sea or find land where he could. I was glad I was not a pilot. We took a course north of Ireland and headed west. A few days later German subs were reported in the area. The convoy split up, every ship for itself. The *Orcades* which was an old ship put on as much speed as it could. I am told it managed 20 knots. At this speed, the ship shook from stem to stern as I can confirm as I lay on my bunk on C Deck. So far as I can remember, it was said that a sub could manage 8 knots when surfaced. We ploughed on – on our own; grey sea and sky, our feelings were mixed. The convoy eventually came back together again and we were to learn that we were heading for Halifax, Nova Scotia. German U-boats had played such havoc with Allied shipping that the only route to the Middle East (our destination) was the one we were taking via Trinidad and the Cape. About a day out from Halifax we spotted a mighty armada coming towards us from the west. This proved to be units of the United States Navy (USN) (they were not then in the War) and they were escorting a convoy of many merchant ships. The USN did a 180-degree turn and headed for Halifax with our troopships. Our escort also did a 180-degree turn and headed east with the merchant ships. I was later to learn that many of these merchant ships were sunk by U-boats.

Chapter 4

Arrival at Halifax, Nova Scotia

We docked alongside at Halifax and in the next couple of days disembarked from the *Orcades* and re-embarked on the troopship USS *West Point*. I was to learn that the *West Point*, 26,000 tons, had been built just before the war as a passenger ship for the north Atlantic run and was then named the SS *America*.

The *West Point* was a different ship from the *Orcades* which had been built for the Australia run and as a consequence had plenty of open deck space. It was the reverse on the *West Point*, weather deck space being very limited, a fact which could have caused us considerable problems. The *West Point* had a crew of 600 and there were 5000 troops aboard. I believe the ship was designed to take 1000 passengers with probably a crew of about the same number. Our Commanding Officer (CO) (Lieutenant Colonel Lilly) being the senior British Officer (apart from a Brigadier) became Officer in Command of Troops (OC Troops) and I found myself detailed to be Ship's Orderly Room Sergeant for which I was paid the grand extra sum of 6d per diem. Yet again, the 1/5 Foresters Orderly Room Sergeant was noticeable for his absence and I think he spent most of the trip on his bunk. A room was allocated about amidships as the Ship's Office; this was off a passageway which ran between two cargo ports, port and starboard. I had a couple of clerks. My accommodation otherwise was not too good, I had a bunk, one of a set three high, on F Deck. F Deck was below the water line and just above the hold. A vertical steel ladder led directly from F Deck into the hold.

It was very hot on F Deck and at night time I took my bedding onto an open deck and slept under the stars, if any. A Ship's Adjutant had been appointed and sent out to join the ship at Halifax on orders of the War Office. He came aboard and was a Captain in one of the Scottish Regiments. He was dressed in tartan trues, a cutaway

4978071 Sergeant E. Roberts,
1/5 Bn. Sherwood Foresters,
C/o Army Post Office 1635,
2 November 41

My Darling,

Everyone here seems to have settled down now, but although the weather has been exceptionally good, lots of the chaps have been ill. However, today most of them appear to have got their 'sea legs'.

The 'Penguins' [books] you gave me have proved to be very useful, in fact I don't know what I should have done without them. From what I can gather the ship's library only contained about 1,200 books, and within a very short time they were all out on loan. Ever since, the general cry has been "got anything to read". I had quite a collection of books, which I packed away in various boxes, but so far haven't been able to find any of the boxes.

The film 'Under your Hat' with Jack Hulbert was shown on board last week. I had seen it months ago, but saw it again; at least it occupied an hour or so.

What we all miss is the entire lack of news, there is no wireless, that is, it is not used. It is under these circumstances that one does really appreciate the value of newspapers and the radio.

So far I seem to have mentioned only the shortcomings of this trip, but of course there are lots of things which help to compensate. Generally the meals are far better than those I have had in the Army to date which I suppose is due to the fact that <u>the normal ship's staff are responsible for the cooking</u>. The Sergeants and Warrant Officers have quite a pleasant lounge set aside for their use, where they can read or write, and at certain times of the day buy beer etc.

I share a cabin with three other fellows, including Jim. This cabin was originally only a single one, but has had an extra three bunks put in. However, there is still plenty of room, and there are adequate facilities in the cabin for washing etc.

Although I am continuing to write letters I don't suppose you will be receiving any for two or three weeks yet, and then no doubt you will be having a bunch altogether.

The 'Jim' mentioned in the letter above was Sergeant W.J. 'Jim' Parker (5050759), an agent for the Salvation Army Assurance Society in Burton-on-Trent and a member of the local Salvation Army Band (see photos).

Excuse the writing, but using one's knee as a table does not exactly aid legibility.

We had a church service on board this morning, you know, the usual army service, which embodies practically all denominations. It was quite well attended, despite the fact that it was a voluntary one, as opposed to a 'parade' service.

Practically anything can be bought on the ship, sugar, biscuits, chocolate and in fact most things which are scarce in England. Only wish I could send a parcel home.

I am looking forward to hearing from you, I should think I shall be getting oodles of letters all at once, and shall have to put them all in date order and start with the oldest.

Yours, with all my love and God bless you,
Eric

service dress tunic and a glengarry. He was immediately christened 'fancy pants', the OC Troops refused to have him as Ship's Adjutant and so far as I know he spent his time on his bunk. The next few days during which the convoy sailed south were spent in settling down and organising our affairs. One of our first enquiries was regarding the Abandon Ship Procedure. There was none and it was left to the troops to organise this. Eventually many of the troops were called upon to perform duties around the ship, even lookout duties, one of the lookout positions was on the top of a dummy funnel and from time to time this was manned by troops.

Numerous Officers and ORs were detailed to assess the accommodation on the ship and the general layout, so that boat stations might be established in the event of abandoning the ship. The amount of weather deck space on the ship was very limited and it emerged that boat stations for most of the troops would have to be between decks with little hope of them getting off the ship in an emergency. There were insufficient life boats or Carley Floats for the troops, after having provided for the crew. The Captain (Kelly) when approached on the subject said that in an emergency he would have cargo nets lowered down the sides of the vessel down which troops might scramble and then into the sea. What the troops would do when in the sea was a matter for conjecture.

There was a daily stand-to on the ship, or 'General Quarters' as the USN called it. The troops were then required to go to their boat stations and the crew went to their various duties. The OC Troops on the ship (Lieutenant Colonel Lilly) was called upon to join the Captain on the bridge. I was instructed to go to the chart room, which was immediately behind the bridge. The Navigating Officer was usually there. The charts were laid out and I found it all rather interesting. At General Quarters the watertight bulkheads throughout the ship were closed. This meant that the passageways which we normally used and which ran from forward to stern were blocked at intervals. This meant that to get to our appointed stations we had to find alternative routes, very often up vertical ladders. All very confusing in an emergency. The Abandon Ship Procedure was eventually formulated and it fell to me to produce thirty or forty copies, of twenty or thirty sheets of foolscap size. It was apparent to me and probably some others that if anything untoward happened we were on a coffin ship – the crew might get away and even I might get away from behind the bridge. I kept my views to myself.

As might be expected, the ship being designed to carry 2000 people at most, the 5600 we now had aboard overloaded the sewerage system. A passageway ran by the compartment on F Deck where I had my bed and this became flooded with sewage. Fortunately there was a fairly deep combing (or sill) to the entrance to the compartment. With the ship rolling rather badly the sewage rushed from one end of the passage to the other. To get out we had to wait until the sewage was at the opposite end of the passageway to the stairs we used and then make a rush for it. Fortunately the problem was eventually solved.

In due time we arrived at Port of Spain, Trinidad. It was very hot and I tried to keep out of F Deck. Judging by the number of pinnaces sailing around in the harbour, some were going ashore. I was not one of them. Refuelling took place and we again set sail south and east. Seas became very rough with waves breaking over the decks of the aircraft carriers in the convoy; the destroyers seemed to disappear under the water. When I was on deck an oiler which had joined us at Trinidad was within a few feet of colliding with our stern. On one day I saw a man fall from a ship sailing parallel a few hundred yards away. A destroyer was detached from the convoy to make a search but was unsuccessful. Many years later I heard that the man overboard was a US sailor who was due to appear before his superior officer in respect of a minor offence. He had just jumped over the rail.

I overlooked mentioning that although we loaded 1001 men onto our two trains at Penkridge and took them all aboard the *Orcades* at Liverpool, when we took the roll on board, we found we were one man short but to compensate we had one man who should not have been with us. The latter man had been medically downgraded; he was a very mild man and was still in a tent when the Battalion was ready to move out. A Company Sergeant Major spotted him, told him to get his kit and get on parade, which he did. It was dark at the time and he was not properly equipped. Apparently en route to Penkridge Railway Station, an Officer volunteered to carry a man's kit bag who under cover of darkness decided to decamp. I never heard any more about him and the Officer arriving at the station put the kit bag on the train. Having transshipped to the USS *West Point* at Halifax, Nova Scotia, a roll call was taken as soon as we were at sea. It was then discovered that one man had skipped at Halifax – I heard nothing more of him but we were now down to 1000 men in the Battalion.

4978071 Sergeant E. Roberts,
1/5 Bn. Sherwood Foresters,
C/o Army Post Office 1635,
3 December 1941

Miss E.M. Lowe
Brook Cottage Farm,
Over Whitacre,
Coleshill, Nr. Birmingham

My Darling
  We are still on the 'ocean wave' and likely to be from the appearance of things. Things are going quite well, despite the arduous task of washing our

own clothing. Actually, although I say it, I am becoming quite adept at washing. Of course I don't vouch for their 'Persil' whiteness, but I like to think this is due to using cold water, and not a reflection on the standard of my labours. At least I have seen clothing on board which is definitely of a dingier shade than my own. Under these circumstances one is reminded quite forcibly of the sterling qualities of housewives and the like. The word drudgery is quite inadequate where referring to the washing of clothing. Fresh water is necessarily rationed on board and this rather adds to one's difficulties.

I should imagine this ship would be the temperance societies' and Salvation Army's paradise, for it is absolutely 'dry'. Actually even this has its advantages, for there are practically no calls on the fellows' purses, that is apart from the purposeless game of 'Lotto'. If you remember, I mentioned this game to you when I first saw it being played at Aldershot.

Since I have been on this ship, I have been employed in the ship's orderly room. It is similar sort of work to that which I have been doing for the past year or so. I understand that if I am very good, I might be given the princely additional sum of 6d per day whilst doing these duties. Judging from this magnificent sum, you will realise what important work it is I am doing. Please excuse all the 'doings'.

Also I might ask you to excuse the writing, for I am lying on a bunk and there is about 18inches clearance between my bunk and the one above. In fact it is impossible to put one's knees up in bed, not that I used to want to, but now I can't I do.

My source of reading matter is becoming strained. I shall have to take the first opportunity of replenishing it. Recently I have been reading things on which I normally should have looked askance.

Letter-writing is certainly becoming more difficult, and considering my present standard, you will be thinking the climate is having an effect on my brain, I wonder? I might write about the colour of the sea and sky, and the rapidity in which the tropical night descends, but if I did I am convinced you would arrive at a definite conclusion concerning my mental faculties, either that, or think I was in a maudlin state (not due to alcohol).

I understand all letters will shortly have to be handed in for censoring. When I hear this I usually start dashing off letters in accordance with my very depleted mailing list, or perhaps curtailed would be a better adjective. They all have the same text, and I am seriously considering, in order to save time and materials, sending one letter with a footnote 'after perusal please pass on to so and so and so and so'. In your case of course I might stretch a point <u>occasionally</u> and send you one all to yourself.

> *Until last night I have been sleeping on the open decks, but I thought I would like a comfortable night's sleep. My bunk is the second one up, and this morning when I was awakened by the bell, being not a little bemused, I couldn't remember whether I was in a bunk or on deck, anyhow I got out 'as on deck' and came the hell of a cropper. The one benefit attached to this display of gymnastics was that when I gathered myself together, I was thoroughly awake.*
>
> *Looking forward to hearing from you (actually dying to). Yours with all my love*
>
> <u>*Eric*</u>
>
> *<u>P.S</u>. Don't you think my attempts at letter-writing are really pathetic?*

Although we got on well with the Americans on board, they seemed to take a poor view of the British and in particular the Royal Navy. The few Royal Navy ships the USN had seen had been involved in Atlantic convoy work and were likely to have been almost permanently at sea. As a consequence the Royal Navy ships were rather battered and rusty. By comparison the USN ships were fresh and newly-painted. As were the USN crew with good quality uniforms, not bleached by time and weather.

On the 7 December 1941, news was received of the bombing of Pearl Harbour [*sic*] by the Japanese and that the US were now at war. We also heard that HMS *Dorsetshire* had sunk a German supply ship in the South Atlantic and the American view of the Royal Navy rose somewhat. So far as I know, a couple of days later part of the convoy, including our ship USS *West Point* arrived off Cape Town, South Africa and I believe the rest 'went round the corner' to Port Elizabeth.

Chapter 5

December 1941: Cape Town, South Africa

By this time we had been at sea about a month and when we went ashore at Cape Town we found walking very odd; I suppose this was a consequence of spending so much time on a moving deck. By arrangement with the shore authority, the coloured members of the USN crew went ashore separately and were taken out of town by bus. Troops and crew went ashore in batches having had some advice from the shore authorities to keep away from *shebeens* (drinking shops) and generally keep out of No. 6 Police District (known as the Malay quarter). I had a map of Cape Town and I suppose many others would have one also. Needless to say, men had to go to No. 6 District and when we left Cape Town a number of men who had been knifed there were in the ship's sick bay. When I went ashore on my first day, I fell in with a man I didn't know but who had a pleasant Irish accent. We saw a couple of ladies leaning against an open-topped car. I suppose they were about 40 and looked very respectable. One said 'Would you like to see Cape Town?' We accepted their offer and were taken onto Table Mount by Rhodes Memorial and could see a line in the sea where it was reputed the Atlantic and Indian oceans met. We had a pleasant trip and were taken to their home where we were given an evening meal. They were both intrigued by my companion's Irish accent. We were told by them that we had been preceded by a Scottish contingent, the members of which had caused quite a lot of trouble in Cape Town and we were warned that we might find our reception generally to be a little cool. Our hostesses kindly drove us back to the docks where we caught a liberty boat back to the *West Point*.

Eric asked one of the ladies, Mrs Jean Beck, to write to Eunice for him as it would not be subject to military censorship; locations could not be communicated to loved ones at all.

> 9 December 1941
> Haslimere
> Hatfield Street
> Cape Town, South Africa

Dear Miss Lowe,

Through our town have passed thousands and thousands of men in convoy during this war. We all consider it a privilege to be able to show the men some hospitality during their leave ashore. In the last convoy I found Eric and his friend 'Wilf'. I am so sorry I did not discover them before dinner as this hotel has an excellent table, they always thoroughly enjoy a meal ashore after weeks of ship's food.

I collected six men that evening in two cars; we took them for a drive round one of the mountains, its name is Lion's Head; does look like it. Their main interest was to see all the lights of the town. Next week we start blackout practices. The Japs have made us realise how we must face the future here too. After the drive we came back here for refreshments and they had to leave for the ship at 11.30 pm.

Eric asked me to write to you, he was looking and feeling very fit and making the very best of everything, he was along with a charming friend 'Wilf', which must make the hundred and one little irritations much easier to bear, if you can share it with a congenial spirit.

Eric was so interested in the serious matters of this country. The native question etc. and we did not have nearly enough time to talk. I wish I could have seen more of him but deliberately did not ask him back, for he was going to trace a Cousin, a bank manager here. I felt sure he would be taken to a pleasant home and have everything to interest him. I do hope the rest of his days were thoroughly happy and interesting.

I am an out and out South African, my ancestors came to this country in 1654, but I have been to England twice, the last time in 1938. I love England, words can never express our admiration for all every one of you have stood up to, may you never have to face such times again.

May the New Year bring all that we hope for most.
>> Best wishes to you and good luck.
>> Yours very sincerely
>> (Mrs) Jean Beck

The 'Wilf' mentioned in the letter above was Corporal Wilfred Harold Wood (4976843). A Derby man who survived the camps and returned home in 1945 (Housley, 1995). Eric and Wilf's friendship endured and continued into the post-war years.

Quite a few of the men were drunk and rather stupid. At the top of the companionway onto the ship, there were both USN and Army Personnel to greet us and I think some of the more recalcitrant spent a night in 'the brig'. The next day I went ashore on my own to investigate Cape Town. I arrived at a point before a high-rise block of offices and whilst I was considering it, a young woman came down the steps and enquired if she could help me. The building was an insurance office and she said she worked there. Then, with rather a hesitant smile, said she was going home, that she lived in a place about 60 miles away named Fisch Hoek, where she lived with her mother. Would I like to go home with her for an evening meal? I spoke about my having to be back on the ship and she undertook to have me back in time. I thanked her and we set off in a very smart electric train to Fisch Hoek. The journey took an hour. She lived in a bungalow on the edge of the town in a beautiful spot overlooking the sea and we had our evening meal on the *stoep*. In conversation I learned quite a lot about the political problems in the Cape, the animosity between the English and Afrikaans-speaking people, not to mention segregation of the coloured people. The coloured people were separated on the train and there appeared to be separate bus stops for whites and coloureds. I duly arrived back at the dock in good time.

On the third day I went ashore with another man and went to Del Monico's. This had a very plush bar and I suppose it was in line with Shepherd's in Cairo and Raffles in Singapore. It had a wonderful ceiling, giving the effect of a starlit night and there were numerous turbaned Indian waiters. We were invited by a rather small man to join him at a table. He was on his own and looked exactly like someone on a holiday in an English seaside resort. It emerged that he was an engineer at a gold mine in Johannesburg and was having a few days' leave. He refused to let either of us pay for anything and then said he had thought of going to a cinema, would we like to go with him, which we did. It was a very fine air-conditioned cinema and of course our friend paid. After the show we thanked our friend and as it was still fairly early decided to see a little more of Cape Town. We walked some distance and it was very hot – we decided to call at a public house for a drink. We discovered that the bar was full of South African soldiers and we were approached by one of them in an apparently friendly manner but it soon emerged that they were looking for trouble. I was surrounded and being jostled, my cap was knocked to the floor and trodden on. Things were becoming grim when suddenly through the street door appeared a USN patrol consisting of a large Petty Officer and two USN Policemen. They were all very large and carried long batons. The three worked the way into the little group surrounding me, the Petty Officer saying 'Hello, what's this? The treaty of Versailles all over again?' They had opened up a gap for me to get out and I thought I might as well go, which I did, and walked back to the docks, followed by the other man I was with.

We were not well informed and assumed we were still on the way to the Middle East via the Red Sea, but what happened was that our part of the convoy proceeded by the Mozambique Channel and then headed for Bombay.

In the Far East, now that France had been knocked out of the war, French Indochina was neutralized. Japanese forces were able to move along the coast from China to Hong Kong, which fell on 25 December 1941. From there the Japanese quickly moved through French Indochina to the Thai border. A formal treaty of alliance was concluded between Japan and Thailand in December 1941. Japan was able to move her forces through Thailand and on to British Malaya.

The Far East command, and particularly Australia, were deeply concerned by the rapid advance of the Japanese forces. Appeals were made to reinforce the principally Australian forces defending Singapore. As a result the destination of the 18th Division was changed from the Middle East to India from where they would sail on to Singapore.

Darling

I found there was no chance of any mail being taken off, so I hung on to the enclosed. It seems a long time since I saw you, like years instead of only a few weeks. They have been good weeks really, although it takes quite a time to shake down and learn the ropes. In fact, I shall be sorry to leave this ship when the time comes. One somehow makes a home of any place one happens to be in for any length of time, and when changes take place they invariably bring about a temporary rupture in a more or less regular existence. Even when one is forced to become accustomed to numerous changes, they are a bit of a nuisance and one becomes tired of continually pioneering into different realms of terrain and conditions. On the other hand of course I should probably be one of the first to wish myself in changed circumstances. I only remember once when I didn't and that was at Penkridge, which so far as I was concerned, was the best station ever.

I shall soon be spending my first Christmas at sea. I imagine it will be a very alien sort of affair. There are far too many people on this ship to have anything in the nature of normal Christmas festivities. I shall have to enjoy myself thinking of last Christmas. I thought it was a bit thick at the time having to play 'happy families', or was that on Boxing day, can't remember, anyhow I shouldn't mind doing it again.

I suppose you will be having a family reunion. Family is the wrong word for I think of it as an army. That may be stretching it a bit, let us say 'a considerable force'. I do hope some of my letters will arrive before Christmas. We have had no mail yet and it doesn't appear likely that we shall have for some time to come. I am certainly looking forward to the time when we get a regular mail service working. Poor old Jim is just about dying to hear from Bette. I am the same for that matter, but not from Bette.

It is now about 9pm and when the ship is 'blacked out' it gets devilish hot below, and anyone right down below just streams with perspiration the whole time. My cabin is on the bottom passenger deck and I consider it is absolutely uninhabitable; I just about spend half an hour out of every twenty-four down there. To give you an idea of how far it is down, when I go onto the open deck to sleep from my cabin, I have to walk up 97 steps. It is a pity they couldn't have made it a level hundred, in fact I have considered asking the Captain what he could do about it, seems a helpful sort of chap.

You will probably find that Bette will be receiving more letters than you, but Jim has nothing much to do other than walk about all day. Whereas I, as usual, have a job to do – all the time. Jim may contradict the statement about his activities, on the other hand he may not consider it worthwhile, probably would involve correspondence stretching a period of years, judging by the rapid exchange of mail at present in existence.

According to the ship's news bulletins, which have become considerably lengthy recently, we seem to be going abroad when things are beginning to hum. The whole business as far as the outsider is concerned becomes more and more complex every day. It is very difficult to determine from the reports received exactly what the allied policy really is. I do hope shortly that there will be some definite clarification of the situation, in order that at least we can see which way we are batting.

I gather that England has been more or less free from air raids, in which we are all more than glad. It is to be hoped that future developments may tend still further to take the war from that part of Europe. It seems queer to be considering England from so far away. In the light of recent experiences England has become considerably reduced in size as in fact the whole world has. One is freed to make adjustments to values, and really it is all together disturbing at times when one allows one's thoughts to wander.

Jim has managed to arrange Salvation Army services on board, at which I understand a fair quota are present. He acts as general factotum, and has I believe 'saved' several wayward souls. I haven't been to any of these services myself, for I think they are quite beyond me. I should confess myself beaten when it came to my lot to holler out 'Are you saved Brother?', and at the same time maintain a straight face and sotto voice. I pull Jim's leg no end, but he takes it all in good part. He is very serious about the whole thing nevertheless.

We still have our regular Church of England services on Sundays, and there are to be various special services on Christmas Day.

Whilst on the subject of Christmas again, according to reports we are to have the normal Christmas fare, turkey and plum pudding etc. But owing to wartime economy there will be no 3d this year, consequently everyone is prostrate with disappointment. However, the prospect of mugs of lemonade may relieve their grief a little.

Sorry if I am going uphill a bit with my writing (which is becoming atrocious), but people are continually disturbing me.

It is now the 24th, and all mail is due in for censoring by today, so I really must put finis to this letter.

Please give my very kind regards to everyone at home.

Yours with all my love,
<u>Eric.</u>

December 1941: Cape Town, South Africa

There had been some confusion at Cape Town, some of the men boarding the wrong ship and there had to be some transfer from ship to ship whilst we were at sea. Between Cape Town and Bombay we celebrated Christmas 1941. We had a very good Christmas meal with turkey and everything to go with it. I understood there was a lot of food left over and went down to the galley to see if I could get a snack. One of the cooks looked round and said you are too late, it has all gone overboard. However, he did find a four-gallon tin partly full of green figs. I had a generous helping of these and they were very good.

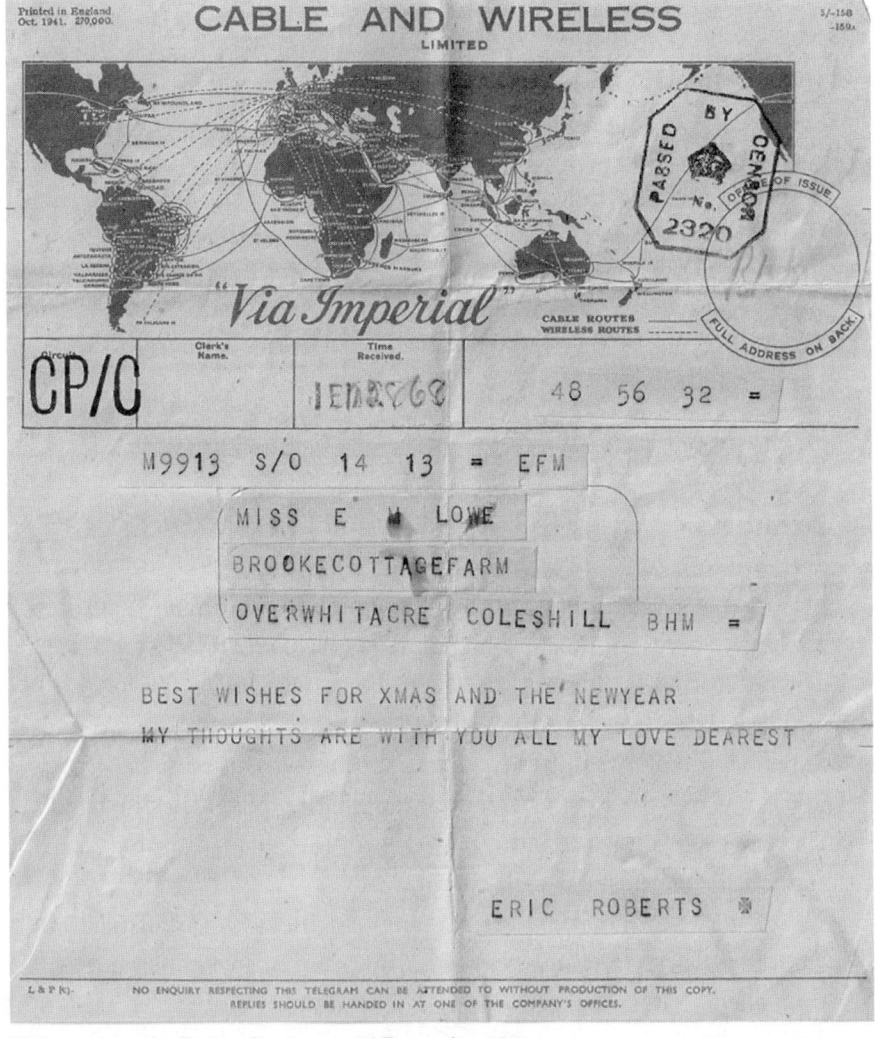

Telegram sent by Eric to Eunice on 25 December 1941.

Chapter 6

1942: Bombay, India and Ahmednagar

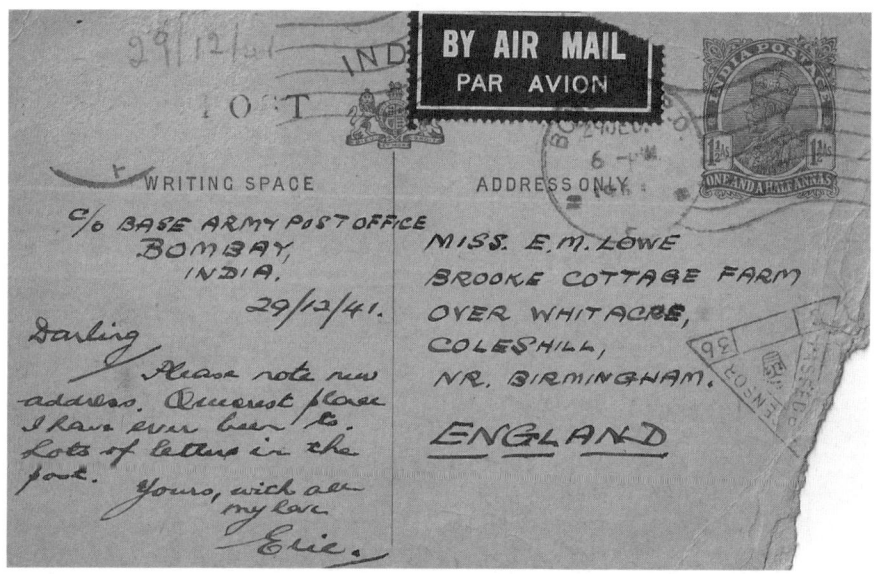

Airmail postcard sent by Eric to Eunice on 29 December 1941.

Arriving at Bombay we had shore leave and I went to see the sights. All very interesting and what I saw made a lasting impression. There were signs of great poverty on the one hand and wealth on the other. Wishing to write home, I went along to the General Post Office, a fine Victorian building. The Post Office was full of people and at the entrance stood a tall Sikh in uniform. He enquired what I wanted. 'A few stamps,' said I, whereupon he took his truncheon and walked towards the Post Office counter banging people on the heads as he went – I followed and a passageway was opened up for me. I obtained the stamps and walked out.

It was very hot and after a sightseeing trip, including an inspection of building works in which very primitive methods were being used, I really felt that I had had enough. I went to a cinema to see an English film. When I came out of the cinema to make my way back to the docks, some of the local people were settling down for the night on the pavement and I found myself stepping over recumbent bodies. Here and there some had *charpoys*, a rough wooden frame with four legs, having hemp string stretched across; I later gathered that a dockworker in Bombay (or some other lowly person) could be born on the street and ultimately raise his family on the street.

Returning to the docks by an archway known as the Gateway to India, a lot of men had gathered to return to their ships. Liberty boats were plying backwards and forwards across the harbour. A boat from the *West Point* arrived – there was a very heavy swell, one moment the boat was level with the dock, then it had fallen about 20'. The method was that when you thought the boat was approaching the top of its movement you stepped out and hoped. Quite a few men had been drinking too much which created a few problems. It was getting late and all were anxious not to be left ashore, so they continued to pile in and when the boat pushed off we were all standing up with our arms round each other's shoulders. There was a maze of lights in the harbour but by some remarkable means the Bosun found his way to the *West Point*, where we climbed up a companionway onto the deck. Some of them were rather troublesome and were bundled off to spend a night 'in the brig' at the behest of either the USN Officer or the Army Officer waiting to receive them.

The following day the Battalion went ashore with all kit and entrained for Ahmednagar which is in Central Province. It was quite a lengthy journey through Poonah and we arrived at our destination the following morning. The countryside through which we travelled was almost devoid of any green leaf. River and stream courses were dried out and everything appeared to be a dusty cream. At Ahmednagar station we were given tea, bread and butter and hard-boiled eggs. We then formed into column of threes and headed for an Indian Army Camp two or three miles away; the five companies followed each other, HQ, A, B, C and D. At the head of the column was the CO, followed by the Adjutant, then HQ Company, in the first rank of which were three men including myself. Halfway down the column was the drum bugle and fife band (an historical British Army combination much preferred to the caterwauling of the bagpipes). The Battalion was dressed with solar topees, khaki shirts and shorts, hose tops, puttees and boots, as well as a full marching order with rifles slung. It was a brave sight, perhaps one reminiscent of days of Empire long since gone.

Sound takes time to travel and although the band was in the middle of the column, the men had difficulty in maintaining step. As one might imagine, the march was hot and dusty, the temperature was in the 90s and when we arrived at the barracks our clothing was black with perspiration. We were greeted with a hutted camp and a lot of Indians were moving around. There would obviously be some permanent staff there and numerous others for menial duties; I was allocated accommodation in what was grandiosely called Viceroy's Commissioned Officers' quarters. I discovered that all the huts were much the same with *charpoys* and little else. The hut floors were raised up about two feet above the surrounding ground to keep water out of the huts during monsoon conditions. My kit was dumped on a bed and I went off to find the Battalion Office. This was on the edge of the camp; there were three offices together, built from concrete blocks, with concrete floors and electric light. They were equipped with tables and chairs. I was concerned with various duties until the early evening when I walked back to my bed. On the way across the parade ground I came across a number of Indians. They were standing around a fire over which was a large metal tank containing boiling water. In the boiling water was a *charpoy* and several more of these were in the vicinity. Apparently, the beds, one of which I was to sleep on that night, were infested with bugs (known in that part of the world as mahogany flats). The boiling process was in an effort to dispose of some of them. I didn't think much of this and so collected my kit and went back to the Battalion Office where I decided to make up my bed on a table. First I ran a lighted match over all the joints in the table to drive out any residents, then laid down my blanket, rigged a mosquito net over it with the aid of some office string and I found that it was not too bad.

There was a canteen in the camp run by a contractor with the exotic name of Wazir Ali. The usual things could be bought there, cigarettes, etc. Bicycles could be hired. I quickly learned a little Hindustani (later known as Hindi). This was a type of soldiers' Pidgin English which had evolved over the years and was then taken up by the Indians themselves for when they were dealing with the English.

Amongst the Indians employed in the camp were *mihtars* (sweepers), *derzis* (tailors), *dhobis* (washer people), *ghari wallahs* (bullock cart drivers) and water carriers. Our washing was collected daily, each item being marked with a *dhobi* mark in Indian ink. Whilst there were 1000 men in the Battalion, all unknown to the Indians our clothing was returned the following day washed and ironed. Some items may have been returned to wrong men but I heard of nothing. There was a village nearby which was immediately put out of bounds. It was possible to hire a two-wheeled trap with a driver. The passenger mounted the trap via a step at the rear and sat with his back to the horse. We had an officer who must have weighed 18 stones, he hired a trap and when he stood on the step, the horse rose in the air with its feet clear of the ground. It was a scrawny animal; the harness broke and the animal fell to the ground. The owner of the carriage went into a paroxysm of rage (or so it appeared), which had to be calmed with a few rupees. [The 18 stone officer may have been Major Barnett. At Singapore, Major Barnett's midriff was split open by a mortar splinter. He was a well-proportioned man and it was later commented that had he been slimmer, he might have escaped unscathed (Housley, 1995).]

4978071 Sergeant E. Roberts,
1/5 Bn. Sherwood Foresters,
C/o Postmaster,
BOMBAY Base, India, 5.1.42

Miss E.M. Lowe
Brook Cottage Farm,
Over Whitacre,
Coleshill, Nr. Birmingham,
ENGLAND

My Darling
  It is now some days since I last wrote to you, and during that time I have collected quite a lot of things to write about, if I can only put my observations and impressions into an interesting form.

Concerning delivery of mail, the service from India to England seems to be rather erratic, and although nothing is laid down as to the length of time involved for delivery to be made, I gather that ordinary mail takes about ten weeks, and air mail approximately one month. In view of this I will, as far as possible, send my letters by air mail. My letters are still of course subject to censorship.

To tell you the truth, I don't relish writing this letter a bit, because as yet I know so little about this country or the people in it, and consequently my opinions have little reasoning behind them, resulting in much contradiction later on. Anyhow, I will endeavour to leave social and political questions alone.

My first contact with India was made at Bombay, whilst we were lying some little distance out of the harbour. From this position the silhouette of the city made a very fine sight, with its queer-looking minarets rising against the sky. In the harbour itself were hundreds of queer-looking craft, lots of them with patched dirty brown sails, whilst others were very trim with shiny paintwork. All these small boats were manned by natives dressed in a variety of costume, some in their own native dress, others in European-style clothing, and quite a lot 'half and half'. Actually the most predominant feature at that time was the smell of the city which was brought to us on the breeze, and I fell to conjecting what it would be like at really close quarters.

Eventually we docked, and I was able to get ashore from about mid-day until one o'clock the following morning. I went ashore with Jim and another chap, and as soon as we passed through the dock gates natives in various states of uncleanliness came from all sides, endeavouring to sell us some useless article at a ridiculous price, women with literally dozens of children in train plucked at our clothing and held out grimy palms for money, beseeching in the whining tones of habitual beggars. Whenever we stopped, small boys tried to clean our boots, or men with long metal instruments wished to clean our ears or manicure our fingernails on the spot. However, after a time, as they saw there was nothing doing, their persistence began to wain, and we were able to proceed in comparative peace, for which I was glad as I was feeling quite weak.

A great variety of odours assailed our nostrils as we passed along the streets, the origin of which we were quite at a loss to place, in fact we were never free from some sort of smell, until at last they became part of the scenery and we failed to notice them so much. In a little alleyway we found a snake charmer with the customary round wicker basket plus cobra. When the chap decided he had sufficient money thrown to him he began to play a small wooden instrument, and the cobra uncoiled himself out of the basket and began to walk, or whatever snakes do, round the circle made by the onlookers. *All very interesting, but so hackneyed.*

The filthy conditions prevalent in the poorer parts of the city are absolutely impossible to conceive; in fact I really don't know how people live at all in such surroundings and in company with so much vermin. There were hundreds of little shops where men sat, in what I should call their shop windows, making shoes, tailoring, beating on pieces of metal, or cooking some weird pottage over a few glowing embers. It was a very queer sight.

In the town proper were some excellent buildings, and quite a lot were in course of construction, being largely built from stone. So far as the building was concerned, the quality of workmanship displayed was very good, despite the rather primitive tools used. I noticed that women were carrying out quite a lot of the 'dirty' work on the building sites, some carrying baskets of rubble on their heads, others sitting on their haunches sorting the rubble out, presumably into various sizes. The stone masons sat around behind matting screens which shaded them from the rays of the sun, and they appeared to be working with amazing speed and dexterity.

After hunting round for a bit, we found a fairly decent restaurant affair, and prices there were similar to pre-war prices in England. The maitre d'hôtel, or whatever he called himself, was very attentive, and anxious that we should have the best attention from his minions, or so it appeared.

When we had finished our meal, we went to the cinema, one which compared very favourably with our London ones, both for size and architecture. I forget the title of the film now, but I know Ginger Rogers was in it. We had a good seat for 1 rupee 8 annas, which is equal to about 2/2d in English money.

After the cinema we ate again, at a different place this time. It was then about twelve o'clock I should think, and the population were going to bed. I say 'going to bed', but most of them seemed to be sleeping in doorways or in the middle of the pavement, in fact we had to thread our way through the bodies. It reminded me of photographs I have seen when towns have been captured and the dead brought out of the houses and laid in rows in the streets. By now, all the small boys had ceased cleaning boots, the men with long metal instruments had ceased cleaning ears, and the itinerant salesmen had almost given up trying to sell their wares. Consequently we got back to the ship with very little trouble, at any rate from the population.

I don't think the picture I have given you of Bombay is at all clear. I feel rather disappointed with my efforts, but it is the best I can do at present.

Also during the afternoon, I sent you a cable, and dispatched several air mail postcards.

We moved from Bombay to our present station, in a military coach as they so lavishly term them. They are very dusty things with hard wooden seats, but I have travelled under a lot worse conditions before.

There was a short march from the railway station to our present barracks, which are native barracks, not British soldiers' barracks. I was allotted a bed in a hut. A hut made from rough timber with matting walls and a tiled roof, and just an earth floor; something like a primitive cow shed less organic matter. I was away from the hut for a time, and when I returned, all the fellows had taken their beds outside and were probing about in the hemp which comprised the top of the bed. I had a look, and there were bugs all over the place, in the cracks and where the hemp crossed over. I had a look at mine and it was just the same, so now I sleep on the orderly room table, at least we have a stone floor here and brick walls. All these various insects were a bit terrible to start with, but I have become accustomed to them now, in fact we have a pet lizard in the orderly room and crickets galore. Actually lizards are rather friendly creatures, and feed on other insects. Our lizard is at present sticking to the door jamb, he usually comes out at about this time of night.

There are lots of other queer animals and birds about, but I shall have to talk about those in another letter.

Nearly all the natives speak a certain amount of English, and dealings with them are not at all difficult. They are usually very respectful, but one has to be firm or they would take advantage of one.

We have quite a lot of native followers, including dhobis (laundry men), moochis (cobblers), durzis (tailors), mihtars (sweepers), and others. In addition there are chaa (tea) wallahs, who produce tea at any time of the day for 2 annas a mug full. There are two kinds of dhobis, the weekly dhobi and the 'flying' dhobi. The 'flying' dhobi takes washing in the morning and brings it back clean and ironed at night, perhaps. The durzi has a hut and several other natives to help him, also a sewing machine. He does a good job and quite cheaply. The mihtars or sweepers are considered to be very low caste, and these men are enlisted in the army as non-combatants, their sole job being to sweep and carry out sanitary. I understand these men are given a small pension after twenty-one years' service. Our particular mihtar is a decent little chap, but he always seems so scared. When he comes into the orderly room he invariably salutes and calls me 'Sergeant Sahib'. I hate all this servility, but I suppose it is necessary. Incidentally, the mihtars are issued with a military uniform, consisting of shirt, shorts, socks, boots and turban.

> *There is a city two or three miles away from the camp, which is out of bounds to us, but we can go to the outskirts where there is a bazaar but very little else. The bazaar is two miles away, and the usual method of transport there is by tonga. A tonga is a thing which is a cross between a rickshaw and a trap, being drawn by a pony. The tonga wallah always tries to get more than his proper fare, sometimes asking as much as three rupees (4/6) for an eight anna (8d) ride, but I think by now most of the chaps are beginning to learn the ropes. The bazaar is nothing very much, only a short street with shops on either side, where one can buy practically anything in the way of food or clothing etc. Fair prices are quoted for goods, and it is a dickens of a job to try and barter these people down.*
>
> *It is winter here now, and temperature averages 90 degrees in day time, and 50 at night. There are only three seasons in India, winter, summer and monsoon. Winter commences in November, summer in March and Monsoon in July. It is not at all hot now, but everything is so dry. Of course there is no grass other than a few brown tufts; the only things which are green are a few stunted trees which grow here and there.*
>
> *Well I think I am about dried up myself, so we will call it a day. 'See our next issue for another long instalment.'*
>
> *Hope this 2000 word epistle won't bore you, but I hope it will give you some little idea of things here.*
>
> *I love you with all my heart and I am just dying to get a letter from you to tell me you are alright. It is hellish not hearing from you for so long. I do hope you are keeping well <u>and</u> happy.*
>
> *Yours eternally with all my love,*
> <u>*Eric*</u>
>
> *P.S. Hope to send you some snaps soon.*

Unless rifles were guarded separately, men were told to keep their rifles with them at all times. We were told that there was a ready market for such things, particularly on the North-West Frontier. The British were warned not to strike any of the locals, but at night time we mounted what was called a prowler guard, when men wore gym shoes and carried pick handles. If anyone was found pilfering, the pick handles were used under cover of darkness.

In the Orderly Room we had two or three lizards which clung to the walls and ceiling. We encouraged these as they were adept at eating mosquitoes. With the Orderly Room being so far away from the camp proper, I didn't bother myself too much about reveille and if I felt like it stayed on in bed a little longer. The Regimental Sergeant Major discovered this (I suppose being told by one of my TA friends) and for a lark at reveille one morning, brought in the drum, fife and bugle band all wearing gym shoes. They stood around my bed where I was sleeping and on a given signal struck up with full force. I am quite sure I jumped clear of the table and came crashing down fully awake.

We were only in India about a fortnight but the Indians have a remarkable bush telegraph. A day or two before we knew ourselves that we were moving, we heard it from the Indians. About to move, we were then faced with settling our affairs at the camp. The Indian men who were working for us came to the Office for a reference and a man was detailed to deal with this. He took a pad of squared paper and proceeded to write upon it such things as 'This man is an idiot.' He eventually ran out of squared paper and when he started to use a plain paper pad, the trouble started, for the Indians thought that a plain paper reference was not as good as a squared paper one.

The 'man detailed to deal with this' was George White (see photos). Corporal George W.C. White (4756254) was Eric's closest friend. George came from Greenwood, Middlesex and was a trainee accountant. He was responsible for managing the regimental accounts as the President of Regimental Institutes (PRI) Clerk.

I usually had my meals on a veranda at the end of one of the huts – food was not good and the meat so tough that I couldn't eat it. The consequence was that any uneaten food I threw out onto the parade ground. Always somewhere in the vicinity were kite hawks which swooped down and caught the food before it hit the ground – I am quite sure they caught the gravy as well.

The letter below is the last letter received by Eunice before Eric was captured at Singapore:

4978071 Sergeant E. Roberts,
1/5 Bn. Sherwood Foresters,
C/o Postmaster,
BOMBAY Base,
India
13 January 1942

Miss E.M. Lowe
Brook Cottage Farm,
Over Whitacre,
Coleshill, Nr. Birmingham,
ENGLAND

Darling

Today I posted a little cloth affair, reputed to be made by hand. I don't have any opinion of my choice or sense of values with regard to such things, but I hope you will be able to adapt it. Owing to present circumstances this cloth was naturally bought in a hurry. Consequently you may shortly be having another 'no mail' period. [According to Eunice's diary, 'Embroidered cloth' was received on 17 April 1942.]

So far as this cloth is concerned, I don't know what the customs duty will amount to, but I have declared the value of the thing in rupees (that is my estimate of the value of it). I do hope the duty will not be too much otherwise it would not be worth sending. I expect it will take at least three months for an exchange of correspondence on the subject.

Today, some of the fellows in the Battalion had mail from England (the first so far), it was composed mostly of air mail postcards, and I noticed the post marks ranged between 12 to 24 November. This of course is no indication as to the length of time for mail deliveries, as things are not yet running properly. It will probably be some weeks before anything like a proper system is able to function.

I think it would be advisable (if you have not already done so) to send an occasional air mail postcard.

So far I have not been in a place where the air graph system functions, that is for outward mail. In fact postal arrangements generally are rather poor, as one might expect.

I sent you a fine letter two or three days ago, but I don't feel capable of writing quite such a lengthy one now. I made a carbon copy of the main part of the letter, and one chap in the office sent it home as it was, and another took extracts from it. In a few days' time I will compile another one to fit in with the one already sent.

I had hoped to send you a snap of myself (p.c. size) with this letter, but time required for an enlargement to be made as soon as I can, although on second thoughts I will send the snap now and an enlargement later. [This was the last photo of Eric taken before the fall of Singapore. It was copied many times.]

Jim is getting along alright and seems to be continually writing letters. He has already made contact with the local Salvation Army.

For the last fortnight, I have eaten more fruit than ever before in my life. Oranges, lemons, tangerines, bananas and lots of other fruits can be bought quite cheaply. I wish I could send you some. The tangerines are my favourites, although they are grown locally and do not emanate from Tangiers.

By the way I worked out the mileage covered since leaving England, and according to my working it is about 25,000 miles, which is equivalent to once around the world. I am quite sure now, that when I do get home, I shall vegetate.

I am really very sorry, but I never remember dates, and I know your birthday is sometime this month, so I wish you very many happy returns. I hope when the next one comes round, I shall be at home?

All the very best.

Yours, with all my love
<u>*Eric*</u>
Please give my kind regards to everyone at home.

As usual, when we were to move, I was sent down to Bombay on the advance party (my TA friends managing to keep in the background once again). I duly travelled down to Bombay by rail and went down to the docks to find the *West Point* there and lying off. I went aboard a tender to go out to the *West Point*. The tender was skippered by a large Indian and I sat by him as he stood by the wheel. I was astonished to see that he had two thumbs and eight fingers on each hand. They had grown in pairs and operated in that way. On boarding the *West Point* I re-established myself in the Ship's Office and did a few odd jobs. The following day, things being rather quiet, I felt justified in having a run ashore. I went ashore with an older man who had served in India for many years. He knew Bombay well and I had an interesting time with him.

The Battalion eventually came aboard and we set sail for what proved to be Singapore. This time we were escorted by the Royal Navy and there was no trouble until we were in the Sunda Strait when Jap planes came over and a bomb was dropped between the two last ships in the convoy. On the deck of the *West Point*, immediately above the Office, we had mounted a British Army light anti-aircraft gun, manned by its British crew. We were gratified to know that this crew spotted the Japs first and fired first; other guns in the convoy following.

At this point there are no further letters home from Eric until 1945. From the Fall of Singapore in February 1942 to August 1945, Eric's narrative is based on his own recollection of events in 1997. Due to his horrific experiences, he had done his best to forget what happened and the pain caused by recalling them, and the night terrors that followed are unimaginable.

Chapter 7

January 1942: Singapore

With air superiority and largely unopposed armoured units, Japan's advance down the Malayan peninsula was relentless. By 31 January 1942, British Imperial forces had formally withdrawn from Malaya, blowing a 21m hole in the causeway between Johore and Singapore.

> We docked in Singapore on the 31st January 1942 without further trouble and quickly disembarked. I gather that during an air raid following our departure, one USN troop ship was bombed and set on fire but later was able to put to sea. On the island we were quartered for the night in a Chinese School [see photos]. However, shortly before we arrived there the Japs had bombed it. We had some food which consisted of diced beetroot, army biscuits, tinned herrings and tea; I didn't think much of this at the time but later such a diet would have been most welcome.

George White recalled that

> We arrived, at the end of January 1942, on the day the causeway linking Singapore Island to the mainland was blown up. 1/5 Foresters Battalion Headquarters, of which Eric was a member, and our Intelligence Section, of which I was one, were located in and around a Methodist Mission Building in a village near to Seletar Aerodrome. We remained there ostensibly, I believe, to defend the aerodrome area (which had no visible defence works) until the night the Japs landed in the north-west of the island on the 8th February. I remember that both Eric and I were on duty on the veranda of the mission when the news of the landing came in – the Japs seemed to penetrate a long way into the island in a very few hours.
>
> The next day we went to a small Chinese village from which I went with one of our Officers into Singapore proper. He went about his

business and I took the opportunity to go into a large department store where business seemed to be as usual. I bought a bottle of 'Old Angus' whisky for the equivalent of 3/6d in Straits dollars. That night at the Chinese village, I sat talking with three other men and I enquired if they had anything to drink. One said he had a tin of condensed milk, so we amalgamated the milk with my whisky and drank it between us.

On the following day we moved again and I found myself on the edge of a rubber plantation. There was some shelling and men dropped into trenches which had been dug. I remember saying 'I don't know what is the matter with you chaps, they are ours.' At that point I was looking across an open stretch of ground across which a truck was coming with our next meal. A shell struck the truck and I dropped into the trench with the others. Unfortunately another man weighing about 18 stones dropped on top of me. This was the man who lifted the trap horse off the ground in India.

For the next few days things were rather confused. The Battalion moved around and occupied various positions. Japanese twin-engined bombers came over regularly, almost to a timetable, and bombed at will. We seemed to have little or no air defences and I didn't see a single British plane. At one stage I was on a side road off the Bukit-Timah road which led north to the causeway which crossed the Johore Straits leading to the mainland of Malaya. [This was most likely Adams Road (see maps).] There was a Jap plane which appeared to be acting as a spotter plane for their artillery. This plane had machine-gunned us and we became a little tired of it. Next time it came over low, without being ordered most of the men rose to their feet, fired at the plane with their rifles and brought it down in flames. The Japs then concentrated their artillery on us.

Later that day I was approached by a Lieutenant who said he had collected 118 men together and I was to go with him a few miles north where we were to man a position across the Bukit-Timah road. The road was straight and the Japs were firing up the road from the north. Most of the men with me had no experience of being under fire and whilst my experience was limited, at least I had some knowledge from my experiences with the BEF in 1940. We duly proceeded north along this road under fairly heavy shellfire. The men in something of a panic were marching in the monsoon ditch to the left of the road and I with rather foolish bravado walked along the road, believing the shells were going over our heads and falling farther south. This was alright until one burst on the road a few yards in front of me. I saw the shell explode and hit the deck. All I suffered was a burn to my upper arm from a piece of shrapnel. I joined the others in the drain.

We arrived at a point where a large pipe from a reservoir on the mainland carried a supply of water to Singapore, crossed under the road, then re-emerged above ground. There was still a fair amount of shelling and sniping and we took up a position in a trench which had already been dug by others. Having taken up our entrenched position by the water pipeline, the shelling continued. They were high-velocity shells and made a noise which I could only describe as that made by a racing car as they came towards us from the north, went over our heads and south. Looking down the road it was possible to see the shells endways on before they passed over our heads. At this stage, the Lieutenant said to me 'You are in charge' and promptly departed – I didn't see him again.

Given the time, location and finality of the last statement, the lieutenant was most likely John Forrester Brownrigg, (71179). He was killed in action on 13 February 1942 in the Adams Road area and is commemorated on the Singapore War Memorial.

I was a Sergeant at the time and one or two of the men were senior to me which made things a little difficult. However, they obeyed my orders and we set up two Bren light automatics on fixed lines on either flank to cover the road ahead. The Lieutenant had said before he departed that there was nothing north of us except the enemy. There was a fair amount of sniping going on around us but it was not possible to know where this firing came from or at what it was directed. I told the men I was with to keep their heads down and hold their fire until instructed. Although I had been placed in charge, there were several there of superior rank to me and one, who was carrying a pistol, in something of a panic, grabbed my rifle and started firing at the trees. So far as I could see this was a waste of ammunition.

As an aside, I carried this rifle from June 1939 to February 1942 and neither with the BEF in France nor on Singapore Island did I fire it; so far as I know this was the only occasion upon which it was fired and not by me. My policy has always been, when necessary, to get my head down, keep quiet and wait for a target. Invariably there would be those who started firing blindly and gave their position away. Much ammunition was wasted.

Night descended and things were rather quiet when I heard the sound of boots on the road ahead. The men were rather jittery and I told them to hold their fire. I shouted out and a voice came back to me with an Australian accent 'It's all right cobber.' It was the better part of an Australian infantry battalion which had come back from the mainland. They stepped over our trench and moved south towards Singapore. During the night the water main was struck and our trench began to fill with water. However, when things were getting a bit too hot for us the Adjutant (Coxon) came and said we were to be relieved, A Company being put in just ahead of us in some trees alongside the road. The Adjutant commented to me that I looked tired and suggested that I should go into an empty Chinese shop to have a rest. I didn't like that but the Adjutant said, 'I will not let you down, if we pull back I will let you know.' He then left with my men. Why he separated me from the other men I will never know but I am sure it was quite deliberate and not in my interests.

To go back a little, when I first joined the Battalion and until we were at Drayton in January 1941, Coxon was then the Regimental Sergeant Major who was an ex-Regular who had been with the 5th Battalion Foresters TA before the war as part of a small group of permanent staff. He was a fairly large upright man who looked well in a uniform but otherwise I couldn't discover much to his credit. After the battalion returned from France in 1940, he was commissioned to full Lieutenant and became the Battalion Adjutant. He was a blusterer and his attitude was that with his long service he knew everything and that men like me should jump to it, do what he said, right or wrong. If it turned out to be the latter, I was to blame; otherwise he would take the credit. He joined the Army as a band boy, not that I held that against him. Regimental Sergeant Major Coxon came to me one morning, when I was typing Part II Orders, and handed me a note for a promotion I was to include in the Orders. It was for the other Lance Corporal (Wood) to be promoted above me to Sergeant. Lance Corporal Wood was one of the original TA men who were at Battalion HQ when I arrived and found everything in such a mess – he did very little apart from the post. I objected to his promotion, mentioning the work that I was doing and had done. Typical of his background, Coxon would not face the issue, saying that was the order and if I had any complaint I should see the Colonel – I think he thought I would crumple. I said I would like to see the Commanding Officer (CO) and that night at about 6.30 pm I stood before Lieutenant Colonel Lilly's desk. I put my point of view to which he listened and I was later promoted to Sergeant. I was duly taken down to the Sergeants' Mess and introduced by a fellow Sergeant. The food was very much better there and for me it was a good move. There was salmon in the river nearby and every day at some time there was salmon on the menu. I didn't concern myself with its origin, just enjoyed it, but I gather it usually arrived by night. For these benefits I paid 3d per day 'extra messing'.

Returning to Singapore, I don't know how long I was asleep in the shop but when I awoke it was getting light and there was an awful clatter outside. The wooden boards I had been leaning against were riddled with holes. I came out of the shop without delay and turned south. I found the CO and one or two others of the Battalion on a tennis court and as soon as I arrived I heard a Lieutenant shout 'Just the man I want, I am going on a recce of the forward Company.' I went back with him the way I had come, by the trench I had occupied during the night (one of our men had been killed and was lying there) and just north we found one of our rifle Companies located in some trees.

The body was most likely Private Claude Louis Mee (4982837) who was a 25-year-old signaller in HQ Company. He was killed in action on 12 February by a single bullet wound above the heart, near the pipeline on the Bukit-Timah road. The body could not be recovered and no burial could be performed. He was married and is commemorated on the Singapore War Memorial (Housley, 1995).

I stood with the Lieutenant I had come with together with the Company Commanding Officer and we were just by the edge of the road – a couple of trees back. At this point a number of tanks came down the road from the north. The Lieutenant said 'I didn't know we had any medium tanks' and at that moment the tanks opened up on us. I dropped to the ground and I was below the tank guns. I was in that position for some time when I realized all had departed, so I picked myself up and ran into the trees with pieces of timber being chipped off around me.

We were never properly armed and it is pointless to fire at a tank with a rifle. My first contact with the Germans and the Japs were with their tanks and we had no defence against them. The Jap tanks moved south from our position by the water pipeline and were eventually brought to a halt farther south by 45lb field guns fired over open sights. I saw no British tanks on the island. Apropos of being armed with useless weapons, at one time I was with an Infantry Officer who had served for four years in the First World War. He told me that in 1914 he was issued with a pistol and fifteen rounds of ammunition. He spent the better part of the war in the trenches and in 1918 returned home with the pistol and the fifteen rounds. My rifle, judging by the condition of it, had also emerged from the trenches in 1918. I might as well have had a peashooter.

Eventually the sound of firing died down and I found a man sitting on a fallen tree who had a bad head wound. He had used his shell dressing but had not staunched the bleeding. I added my shell dressing and he said to me, 'If you will help me I will lead you out of this lot.' Apparently he was a man of the 1st Leicester Regiment and had been stationed in Singapore for some time. He knew the area. We moved through a swampy area and found a road, also by a stroke of luck an Army lorry came along which we got on and later delivered the wounded man to a small Military Hospital. The lorry moved on into the centre of Singapore where I left it to see if I could contact my Battalion. I was soon in the middle of a heavy air raid and dropped into a trench with a miscellaneous collection of other men. We were being bothered by a Jap plane which came over the area several times machine-gunning. Next to me was a large Sikh; he rose from the trench with a Boys Anti-Tank Rifle to his shoulder, fired at the plane as it went over low and brought it down. I didn't think such a thing was possible.

A short time later I spotted one of our men with a truck, he had come to pick up stragglers and I hastily got aboard. I found the Battalion in position on a small hill and it was rather quiet at the time. I enquired of a friend of mine if there was anything to eat and he produced some currants in his steel helmet. Shelling started again and it seemed that they were ranging shots. Fortunately we were relieved by another regiment who occupied the same position but unfortunately by then the Japs had found their mark. The relief suffered quite heavy casualties.

George White noted that

from there, after much confusion including the sighting of a Jap tank, the unit retired to the vicinity of Adams Road, which crossed the Bukit-Timah road. Battalion HQ took possession of a large house sheltered by an incline behind it. Here for a day or two we remained, Eric mainly supporting Lieutenant Colonel Lilly and I with what remained of the intelligence section (we had a motorbike, which caused two or three accidents to our number). We were occupying part of the front line and there were a good many alarms etc.

No one seemed to know what was going on but I remember at one stage being in a bungalow which was being used as Battalion HQ when we had a message indicating there was to be an official escape party from the island on a naval vessel. We were to send either four or six men of various ranks. The CO's eyes fell on me and he said 'No, not you, you are too useful.' I learnt later that the escape party got to India where they spent the rest of the war in comparative comfort. Behind the bungalow, A Company had established a defensive position and in the bungalow garage a Regimental Aid Post was set up and there were several wounded there, including two or three Japs who had been brought in but had died. It was rather hectic there; we were being heavily mortared and overnight, through an artillery liaison officer, we tried to get artillery SOS defensive fire but no luck. There was no water in the bungalow but there was a water standpipe by the road some fifty yards away. At first light I went out with a number of water bottles and crawled to the standpipe and reached up, only to find that it was dry. So we had to go thirsty but later on when the mortaring became worse, the Adjutant said to me that he thought we had better go across the road.

Unfortunately, the members of A Company who were entrenched behind the bungalow spotted us, left their positions and headed south towards Singapore. About then the CO came back, having been elsewhere. He was furious and the three of us ran down the road to get the men of A Company back. They were eventually stopped. There was heavy shelling at the time but the CO insisted on forming the men up in threes on the road and marching them back into their previous position. I was detailed to follow in the rear and shoot anyone who broke ranks. I had a round in the breech but fortunately no one broke ranks. A Company went back into their position but not for long; the position could not be held. Confusion reigned and at one point I found that I had collected around me a group of men. I had a Bren gun and I was being followed by a man with a box of ammunition. We moved south from building to building, taking cover as we went. We arrived at a very high steel fence which surrounded Government House. This was the point when twenty-four Jap twin-engine bombers came over to bomb Government House. They dropped their bomb loads and I remember being lifted clear of the ground. We had no casualties but I remember an old tank belonging to one of the Indian Regiments being set on fire and one of the occupants was hanging dead from the turret.

The tank was part of a light tank squadron from India that arrived with Eric's 18th Division. They were the only tanks to reach Malaya. The Garrison Commander Lieutenant General Percival described them as being obsolete and had been collected from training establishments in India. Several had to be repaired immediately before they could be used (Percival, 1949).

By some remarkable means, I found myself back with the bulk of the Battalion in the Botanical Gardens. Entrenched positions had been dug there by the Aussies. We occupied these trenches and discovered they had abandoned quite a lot of food and clothing. By now things had quietened down and we were out of contact with the enemy. During the night there were many explosions, which I discovered were due to our men 'spiking their guns'. This was achieved by putting a round in the breech and another round in the muzzle of the gun. By these means the gun barrel was split and made useless. I imagine it was as well to stand clear when the gun was fired. When it was light the CO went off to see what was happening, he had a man with him and they were seized by the Japs and disarmed. He was told that Singapore had capitulated the day before. He returned to us with the sad news and we later received instructions to pile our arms without damage and close upon our B Echelon. This was our rear base where we had our ammunition and other supplies. I am afraid from our rifles we removed the bolts and tossed them into a stream so that they would be useless.

By the late afternoon I arrived at our B Echelon where I established myself in the back of a truck to receive information about what had happened to members of the 1/5. Men were coming throughout the night and I sat there throughout the night. In the end it emerged that the Battalion had lost twenty percent of its strength, missing, killed and wounded (200 men). This between landing at Singapore on 31 January 1942 and the capitulation of the island on 15 February 1942.

Actual losses were in reality much lower. Housley (1995) stated that 5 officers and 59 ORs were killed during the defence of Singapore with 2 unarmed officers shot illegally (murdered) following the surrender; however, given the confusion following the surrender it's likely that the remaining 134 were unaccounted for or 'missing' at the time.

The Japanese demanded unconditional surrender and in the interest of saving lives, the Garrison Commander General Percival accepted. On 15 February 1942 more than 80,000 men laid down their arms. As Churchill was later to write '…it was the worst disaster and largest capitulation in British history' (Churchill, 1951).

Chapter 8

Home Front: February–May 1942

News of the surrender of Singapore was announced by Churchill on the evening of 15 February 1942. However, because serving soldiers were unable to disclose where they were or where they were going, the fate of the men of the 1/5 Foresters was completely unknown to their relatives.

Private Danny O'Brien had been with the 1/5, but was selected for wireless training and transferred to the Royal Signal Corps. He was still in training in England when the 1/5 landed on Singapore Island. Knowing the 1/5 was part of the 18th Division, he knew from newspaper reports that the regiment had been in action at Singapore and were now likely to be prisoners. Danny sent a letter of sympathy to Eric's parents and Aunt Lilian. He didn't realize that this was the first indication that Eric may have been captured.

18 Mannville Terrace
Bradford
London Address (Home)
21 Eastminster
London
24-2-42

Dear Mr & Mrs Roberts & Eric's Aunt
Last Monday week I saw the news in the papers that the unit had been in action in Singapore and I was horrified to think they had been sent there nearly direct from England.
May I offer my sincere sympathy with you today, especially as there has been no news although today's statement in parliament that 73,000 had been taken prisoner is good news and I am sure that Eric was one of that number.
As perhaps you know I didn't go with them as I was due to go on a wireless course, but I can't forget all my old pals in the 1/5 and the good times we all had in the orderly room.

> *Today by a coincidence I had a card from Eric posted in India; yesterday I had a letter from Wilf Wood posted in S. Africa. But at the moment of course I can't reply but I want to as soon as possible so please let me know when you are informed of his whereabouts. My home address will always find me.*
>
> *When I think of all my pals and some since the day I joined who are now prisoners for God knows how long it makes me hate this business. These lads were only army pals and yet I was very upset upon hearing the news so I can truly sympathise with you all. Will you also tell Eunice how sorry I am.*
>
> *Praying that we shall have good news soon.*
>
> *Believe me*
>
>

Yours very sincerely
Danny O'Brien

>
> *P.S. I don't know whether Eric's Aunt (I don't remember her name. Do you remember the day I brought his bike home?) knows Cyril Taylor's parents. If so would you kindly tell them one of his pals sends his sympathy.*

Private Cyril John Arthur Taylor (4978065) lived on Burton Road, Burton-on-Trent. He was a close friend of Eric's but was never mentioned to the family again. Cyril was killed in action at Singapore on 12 February 1942 and is commemorated on the Singapore Memorial. He was 23. By the time Danny wrote the letter above, Cyril was already dead. It would be more than a year before his parents were notified.

Aunt Lilian forwarded this letter on to Eunice who recorded in her diary: '27 February, had a letter from Mrs. Degg on arrival which completely bowled me over. She enclosed letter of sympathy from Danny as he had read the report in the papers that Eric's unit had been in action in Singapore.'

In the absence of any official information it was left to individuals to find out what they could. Officials would only provide information directly to next of kin. This put Eunice and Aunt Lilian at a disadvantage, Eunice being Eric's fiancée and not his wife and Lilian his aunt. Undaunted, Eunice began a long campaign to find out what had happened to Eric. She saved a copy of her first appeal to the prime minister from March 1942.

> Brook Cottage Farm,
> Over Whitacre,
> Colehill,
> Nr. B'ham.
> 4/3/42
>
> To:
> The Rt. Hon. Winston Churchill C.H.M.P.
>
> My Dear Prime Minister
> I realise that I am taking a great liberty in writing to you, but trust that you will understand why I am making this endeavour to enlist your sympathy when I explain my dilemma. Since the fall of Singapore we have received no news of the troops there and although I have seen reports to the effect that the Sherwood Foresters were there, I am unable to find out whether the 1/5th Bn. (Infantry) was in action. My fiancé no. 4978071 Sergeant E.B. Roberts is in the H.Q. Coy of this Battalion and I am striving to carry on bravely in my job (Civil Service) whilst suffering great anxiety on his behalf. If there has been any recent information I should esteem it a very great favour if I could be notified under cover of the stamped addressed envelope enclosed.
> Thanking you in anticipation and assuring you of my loyalty at all times. I am, my dear Prime Minister,
> Yours respectfully,
> Eunice M. Lowe (Miss)

However, the response provided no information and simply referred her to the War Office. The War Office, in turn, could provide no further information.

> Miss E.M. Lowe
> Brook Cottage Farm,
> Over Whitacre,
> Coleshill,
> Nr. Birmingham
>
> Dear Madam,
>   In reply to your letter of 6th inst. It is regretted that owing to the difficult conditions prevailing in the Far East I am unable to give you any definitive information at present regarding No. 4978071 Sergeant E.B. Roberts, 1/5th Sherwood Foresters.
>   Every effort is being made to obtain accurate information and when such is received, his next-of-kin will be at once notified.
>   Trusting you will receive reassuring news in the near future.
>   Yours faithfully,
>   J Baines <u>Major</u>
>   For OFFICER I/C INFANTRY RECORDS.
>   York. 9.3.42.

Eunice then contacted the British Red Cross. They could provide no news and were unable to even confirm whether Eric was in Singapore at all. The Infantry Records Office in York was at least able to confirm that Eric had been serving in Singapore. However, as they had received no casualty report, it was possible that Eric may have escaped.

> To:- MISS E.M. Lowe   Date 10.3.42
>   BROOK COTTAGE FARM
>   OVER WHITACRE
>   COLESHILL, NR. BIRMINGHAM
>
> ~~Sir/~~Madam,
>   In reply to your letter of <u>4. 3.42</u> I am directed to state that no report of a casualty has been received in this office in respect of <u>4978071 SGT. E.B. Roberts SHERWOOD FORESTERS</u> who, according to the latest record available, was serving in
>   ~~Malaya~~

> Singapore.
> Your anxiety regarding the ABOVE NAMED is fully appreciated and every endeavour is being made to obtain news of him but, in view of the difficulties arising from the capitulation of Singapore, it may be some time before information is forthcoming.
> You may rest assured that any news received will at once be communicated to ~~you~~ HIS NEXT OF KIN.
>
> I am,
> ~~Sir~~/Madam,
> Your obedient Servant
> A.E. Glinton Lieut.
> For OFFICER I/C INFANTRY RECORDS, YORK

In the absence of any official information, relatives were given to wild speculation concerning the fate of their loved ones. The improbability of sending men to Singapore knowing full well that the island could not be held gave the families some hope that the 1/5 were never there at all. Aunt Lilian expressed such theories in a letter to Eunice:

> 62 Eton Rd.
> Burton-on-Trent
> 13-3-42
>
> Dear Eunice
> Many thanks for yours of this morning – Yes, I quite understand you were waiting for news; and when I got it you may imagine I felt in despair. But I have been alternating between despair and hope since the first intimation from Danny; and I must say that after going over and over all the possibilities I had really begun to feel more hopeful. I had just remarked to Aunty Rose this morning about it being Friday and also the <u>13th</u> just when your letter arrived. Of course I was at once plunged into the depths; but hope springs eternal in the human heart, and by this afternoon, I am beginning to scramble to my knees and get back into the ring (as it were), and to feel that we must not allow ourselves to be knocked out yet.
> Ronald was here on Tuesday and of course Eric is the main topic of conversation, and Ronald will not have it that Eric even <u>got</u> to Singapore.

He says the journey from where Eric was when he last wrote was at least 3 weeks by <u>sea</u>; and that would make it a little over a month between the date of your last letter and the <u>fall</u> of Singapore. Mr Churchill himself stated in the house that they knew <u>3 weeks</u> before, that they could not possibly hold out, they had insufficient <u>water besides stores of all</u> kinds. So assuming that Eric went immediately to Singapore after writing you on Jan 13th it would only leave a week or 10 days in between; and it would be almost <u>unbelievable</u> for them to plunge fresh reinforcements in at that late hour. In fact, simply <u>throwing</u> men away. Now – a few days ago I read in the Daily Herald an article about the fall of <u>Java</u>; in this the writer was showing how the fall of Java was largely due to Singapore failing to hold out longer and mentioned about large reinforcements being on their way to Singapore which <u>had to be diverted elsewhere!</u> All this makes one think. I am now wondering <u>where</u> you got the information that Eric's Company was actually at Singapore, also I am inclined to the idea that the replies that you have so far obtained are just the ordinary routine ones sent out to all and sundry.

We know <u>something</u> of office routine and no doubt the War Office and all these other organisations are daily receiving thousands of enquiries. It would seem therefore we must just <u>wait and still hope</u>. The longer we go without official news the more hopeful it may be.

This week in our local paper there have been two Burton boys whose parents or wife have received news, one is reported missing as from Feb 15th at Singapore and the other wounded and in hospital. These boys had been in the Army sometime – one of them 6 years but I don't suppose that would make any difference. Mr. Shaw (next door to us) says he wouldn't be surprised to find Eric has gone to Australia. Wouldn't it be grand if we could find that were true? And another thing – a few <u>escaped</u> from Singapore, and if our Eric had half a chance he would not be slow to make the best of any advantage. What about his friend Jim? Has his wife any information?

With regard to our 'Mail' I wrote again and asked if they would kindly reply to our enquiry. They have just ignored it. The fact is <u>they don't know</u> and I think no one else does either yet. One thing we can rely on if Eric has any chance, wherever he is, he will try and let us know something as soon as he can. <u>We must simply try not to think the worst. I don't.</u> At the very least we shall live in a constant state of <u>strain</u>.

Thanks very much for the typed addresses I shall have quite a stack. No it won't be any use sending parcels until we have more news. You may depend I shall let you know as soon as I receive any. You know even the War Office isn't always right and if Eric and company went to Singapore and were afterwards diverted elsewhere – they may even have got records of troops as being in action at Singapore who didn't actually reach there. What do you think about these ideas? Is there any reasonable grounds for optimism, or is it just wishful thinking?

I think that accounts of the Hong Kong atrocities were simply appalling, but we <u>can't</u> think that is going to happen everywhere. One hears so many conflicting accounts, it is the same with the Germans, but some of their prisoners say how well treated they are. As you say we must hope and pray. I am glad to know your religious convictions are a comfort to you. We do have to try and trust that all may turn out for the best, but it is sometimes very hard to see why an <u>Almighty</u> God <u>allows</u> the evil which is in the world. Write me again, trusting we may both be speedily relieved of our worst anxieties.

With much love.
L. Degg

P.S. No, I do not think you could possibly do more than you have done, at any rate for the present. I think you have done all possible and I am sure it has been a real help and comfort to me to know you have taken it off my shoulders for while I have been so poorly I have felt quite unequal to it and I am singularly short of anyone else to help in these matters. I wrote one long letter and one postcard to Eric since you were here but I feel I don't know how to write until I hear something more. I fear he will be upset if he has had nothing from us, yet it is all a big problem, but I will write to him again soon if I hear nothing more.

Following Aunt's suggestion, Eunice contacted Jim Parker's wife Bette. Bette still believed that the 1/5 were in India. She was unconcerned and could see no connection with Singapore.

21 Glasgow Rd.
Paisley,
Scotland.
15.3.42

My dear Eunice,
   Ever so many thanks for your letter which I received at the beginning of the week. The last letter I received from Jim was dated round about 29 December.

I haven't sent any postcards, but I will do. Incidentally I received a card from Jim containing three silver leaves, it's really very <u>pretty.</u>

Yes I still number my letters. Today's number of 31. No Jim doesn't say very much about the barracks, he only says they are expecting to move shortly. Exactly what do you mean about Singapore? Are you worrying about them going now, or did you mean if it had been there instead of India. I shouldn't think you need worry about that now. No. 9 haven't had any recent cables.

Yes I wish we were a little nearer so that we could have a good old chat. I am on the phone, and I have your phone number if at any time I need you urgently. Jim was saying that he went with Eric and a friend as far as the pictures, but didn't go inside. Instead he went to the Army (Salvation). Well I am going to two 'coming of age' parties next week; both girls are in the songsters.

I expect Birmingham is still very much the same. Have you had any Air Raids lately, I hope you haven't as I think Birmingham has had more than enough.

Well Eunice, for today it will have to be cheerio.
Write soon. God Bless.

Sincerely yours
Bette

Aunt Lilian continued to live in a state of strain and extreme anxiety. Her husband Jim had died suddenly in 1939, her son Ronald married and moved out in 1938 and Eric was called up in 1939. Within the space of two years the house was empty, the country was at war and Eric's fate was a mystery.

62 Eton Rd.
Burton-on-Trent
20th Mar 42

Dear Eunice
Many thanks for yours of this morning with enclosure. I am replying at once as I intended to write anyhow this weekend. I received the enclosed from the 'Mail' office the other day – but as you will see it is of no use to us – they have been a dickens of a time saying <u>nothing</u> haven't they? I wrote a second letter over a week ago so we can rule them out now. I am not really surprised for I

don't expect they know anything about the matter, certainly not as much as we know ourselves. I received a postcard from Eric on Tuesday, similar to yours except that someone had scratched out the date with a knife. I am glad yours was intact – evidently they were sent at the same time. Now really we know that as late as 17 January Eric was still in India, however, we can assume that they moved on soon after that. Well if the journey to Singapore takes three weeks it only leaves one week before Singapore surrendered. It certainly doesn't sound likely to me that they would land a lot of men so late in the day does it? And especially as Mr Churchill said they knew they could not hold it <u>three weeks before</u>.

I wish I had saved that article I read and which I told you of before, in which the writer stated that large re-enforcements on the way to Singapore were diverted elsewhere as they were too late to save the situation. It was a similar article to this you have sent me but at the time I didn't think to cut it out. That is why I am clinging to a forlorn hope; anyhow it is just as likely Eric might have been with that lot as that he was with this mentioned in <u>your</u> cutting. And anyhow would they call Eric's Company a <u>half trained lot</u>? I think they could almost be called old campaigners except of course for the climate.

[On arrival, Lieutenant General Percival judged the 18th Division to be 'fit, but soft' (Perceval, 1949). This is hardly surprising given the many months at sea and limited combat experience.]

Like you I am longing to have some definite news of some kind just even if Eric is not at Singapore he may not have been able to write or cable for a while after sending those postcards and as we have only <u>just</u> received them we have still a chance of something coming in the next few weeks. If we hear nothing at all, I shall then begin to think he is a prisoner of war. In this case I suppose it may be <u>months</u> before we receive official notification. But if we could hear of him being fairly treated etc., I am not sure that this might not be for the best – he would at least be out of the fighting, whereas we shall never know <u>where</u> he is or what he is going through. Oh dear, I keep on turning it all over and over in my mind until I feel I shall go crazy (even more crazy than usual I mean). I think I will write him another long letter in which I will tell him all we have heard of our 'Bob' and how anxious his Aunty and others are etc. <u>He</u> would know who 'Bob' was but the letters are censored we couldn't speak of his movements at all. Yes it seems awful for him not to have had any letters in all this time; it makes me feel wild. The worst of it is, that if the enemy has got him, he won't stand a chance of getting anything for a long time, otherwise he might have got some of them by now.

Many thanks for offer of the snap. No he hasn't sent me one and I haven't heard of his mother having had one. But I could have some printed if you would lend me the negative and you must let me pay the cost. I am quite anxious to see it. By the way, before I go any further I must tell you that I found a postcard from you in our outer letterbox Tuesday this week – it must have been there over a week and I expected you would wonder why I had never acknowledged it. It had stuck flat on the side of the box and although I feel in there regularly I had missed it; eventually it fell out with a paper which had been pushed in.

I note your information re Eric came from the Records Office and it would seem to be authentic information but there are lots of errors even normally and it might possibly be that they were posted as serving in Singapore before they actually arrived there and if once more they were among those diverted elsewhere. Army records would need this correction. Another thing I feel curious about is what would the Japs do with all those 63,000 prisoners? Would they be kept at Singapore or taken to Japan? I should think it more likely to stay where they were, shouldn't you?

Oh what a problem. I am rather surprised Jim's wife has had so little news. It would seem she has had less than us, then (very queer) but of course if it had not been for Danny O'Brien, we should have been just as ignorant of Eric having arrived from India. We should also have been saved a lot of anxiety. Shall you tell her all about it? I hope she will let you know if she gets any news first. I haven't seen Ronald just lately so he doesn't know our latest about Eric. I expect he will be coming in soon. It is his birthday today, but isn't the weather miserable again?

But I must bring my rambling to a close now. Cheer up and hope for better news soon. If I hear anything be assured I will at once let you know.

Lots of love,
Yours affectionately
L. Degg
P.S. Stamps are what I owe you.

A reply arrived from Danny which seemed to confirm that there was no mistake and that the 1/5 Foresters were at Singapore when it surrendered.

> 18 Mannville Terrace
> Bradford
> London Address (Home)
> 21 Eastminster
> London E1
> Tues
>
> Dear Eunice,
> I am so sorry that my letter was the first intimation you had of Eric and the lads. My information about the war there reached me through the News Chronicle and Daily Express of 16 Feb. Between them they said the 18th Division comprising the 53th, 54th and 55th Infantry Brigades were at Singapore. Well the 55th Infantry Brigade was our one. The papers also mentioned names of Regiments there, but of course did not give Battalion numbers. The Sherwood Foresters were mentioned.
> So you will see I am pretty sure and so is my pal, at the moment in Gainsborough who left the unit at the end of September. You should now write to the War Office Casualty Dept. and ask for news. Give rank, name and No. and unit. My pal Jack Reading wrote to me today and tells how he was upset for a week by the news. He was as much a member of the Office staff as anybody.
> I am so sorry but that's no help. By the way, write to the Derby Evening Telegraph. They might have some information. I would have replied yesterday but for the fact that we had our last written exam today and I was very busy swotting. I shall be leaving here next week so if you write again, will you please send it to my home for forwarding.
> Eunice I am confident that the lads are prisoners. Over 60,000 were taken and that appears to be nearly all the garrison. Some were evacuated but only a few. The casualties were small so I really do think that most of them are now in Jap hands.
> I know you will realise that I am anxious for news so should you get any will you please let me know. I do hope Mrs Degg and Eric's parents believe that he is safe, and I very much regret that I should have broken the news. Should I find anything fresh I'll let you know. Have been scanning the papers since that Monday.
>
> Yours very sincerely
> Danny O'Brien

The confirmation from Danny came as a shock to Aunt Lilian. However, although the 1/5 Foresters had been captured, with no official confirmation that Eric had been taken prisoner, there was a possibility that he had managed to escape. Aunt Lilian began to hope once again.

> 62 Eton Rd.
> Burton-on-Trent
> 26-3-42
>
> Dear Eunice
> Thanks so much for your letter of yesterday and for sending me the War Office notification. As you remark the only bit of comfort (so far) is the news that Eric has not been posted as a casualty. And each day that passes without <u>that</u> news will make us feel a trifle reassured. Especially as there have been (to my knowledge) some few Burton boys' relatives who have recently had these official letters of their being missing and worse. I enclose one of these as a sample for you to see. I had intended going to this address to see if I could gain any information but sorry that so far I have been quite unable to get as far, also I doubt we should be an atom forwarder. I think now that we know as much as we shall do for the present and I watch but eagerly with a vague idea of getting <u>something</u> from Eric and shall not quite give up this possibility for some time yet. I <u>cannot even now</u> altogether take it as <u>certain</u> that Eric was at Singapore. It is very queer but it despite all these official assurances that he <u>was</u>. Of course I have simply nothing but <u>intuitions</u> (good word that) to account for this.
> Yesterday – in which it seems my sister [Eric's mother] seems to have now quite accepted it that Eric <u>was</u> at Singapore but she still spoke of a case she knows of near her, a Sergeant Major, who was at Penkridge and departed with the unit when they went away. It seems his relatives had a cable from <u>him</u> last Friday saying he was quite OK and they gathered he had escaped from Singapore with 11 <u>Officers and men</u>, but where the cable came from I don't know and really all these inklings including the cases you speak of as having got away makes me wonder if Eric may prove to have also been amongst a <u>lucky few somewhere</u>. I am sure of this, <u>he</u> would leave no stone unturned to make the very best of any opportunity, that is of course if he had the remotest <u>chance</u>. Also I know he would write or cable to some (or all) of us if he was able. But as we don't know what the circumstances may be and every case different, we must still hold on to that hope that something may get through to comfort us. We have never as yet got even an airmail letter under 2 months have we? So

> we could not expect any ordinary mail before about the middle of April. If only we knew he was being well treated I wouldn't mind so much the thought of him being a prisoner.
>
> I quite understand your reluctance to speak the news to your friend Bette, but of course there is no alternative is there? And if in the meantime <u>she</u> collects any information she will then pass it on to you. I have not written to Eric for about a fortnight. I seem to be waiting for something to turn up (like Mr. Mcawber) so that I should have something to write about. In any case I don't think there is much chance of Eric receiving letters as things are, so a little delay can't make much difference can it?
>
> Thanks so much I shall be very glad to see the snap of Eric. Oh well, once more I will stop. I have been sitting doing this in between getting a bit of dinner ready, this was to make sure I got it written well before post time. Hoping this finds you well and as hopeful as possible. Eric always said – keep your chin up. So until we are finally defeated we must endeavour to do so, eh?
>
> Lots of love
Yours affectionately
L. Degg
>
> P.S. In tonight's paper 6.00pm more official notices of local lads missing. One is mentioned as being in the Sherwood Foresters and serving in Singapore. There is also an advert in the Personal Column asking the lady friend of 'Taffy' Sherwood Foresters and his soldier friend to communicate with – then follows an address at Rollestone. Oh dear, I shall now <u>dread</u> the postman – it seems to have taken away my last hope.
>
> What do you think now?

As Aunt Lilian describes above, the names of 'missing' soldiers were beginning to appear in local newspapers. These were placed in the papers by families and were not official notifications posted by the authorities. When the details of Captain Norman S. Thorpe (75410) and Second Lieutenant Michael T.T. Stephens (180256) appeared in the *Burton Mail*, there was sufficient detail in the descriptions for Eunice to be able to contact the parents of both men.

> Lancaster & Thorpe
> Ophthalmic & Sight Testing Opticians
> 100 St. Peter's Street
> Derby
> 28th Mar. 1942

Miss E.M. Lowe
Brook Cottage Farm,
Over Whitacre,
Coleshill,
Nr. B'ham.

Dear Miss Lowe,
    I am afraid that you can take it as quite definitive that the 1/5th Battalion Sherwood Foresters was at Singapore, as my Son was attached to C Company of that Battalion, and my Son also was at Bombay at the end of December. A large number of the local men belonging to this Battalion are now being posted as missing, that being the only information the War Office have at present. However, this does not mean that we shall not hear in due course that they are safe and Prisoners of War.
    Hoping that when definitive news has reached you it will be good news, I beg to remain,

> Yours faithfully,
> B. Thorpe

> March 28 1942

Dear Mrs Lowe,
    Thank you for your kind letter expressing sympathy with the situation regarding my Son Second Lieutenant M. Stephens. He is attached to the 1/5th Sherwood Foresters and I think there is little doubt that your fiancée sailed on the same boat at the end of October.
    It is a serious business, but in as much I am led to believe that the Foresters were the last to set foot in Singapore, there is ground to hope that they barely reached the fighting line. We are quite hopeful that we shall learn that our boy is a prisoner and although that is not by any means a pleasing prospect it will

> *at least give us hope of seeing him again. I hope with all my heart that your fiancée is safe. It is all the worse after being in France.*
>
> *I understand that <u>when</u> the Japanese send the lists of prisoners it will be in Japanese language and will then have to be dealt with by interpreters and translators, thus prolonging the time and waiting.*
>
> *I sympathise deeply and pray fervently that both of them will be spared and that the present strain will shortly be relieved by some encouraging information.*
>
> *Yours sincerely,*
> *A.T. Stephens.*

Although both Captain Thorpe and Second Lieutenant Stephens survived captivity, Captain Thorpe had more eventful experiences. Having been captured at Singapore, he was transferred to Formosa in October 1942 and then to Shirakawa Camp, Japan in 1944, and from there he was sent to Mukden in China which was liberated by Soviet forces in 1945. He returned home in November 1945 via Hawaii, San Francisco, Vancouver and New York. By the time he was back in England, he had travelled once around the globe (Housley, 1995).

Then at the end of March 1942 Aunt Lilian received official notification that Eric was posted as 'Missing'. This meant that the army no longer had any record of him. The notification confirmed nothing and Eric could potentially be an escapee, a casualty, a prisoner of war or dead.

> *62 Eton Rd.*
> *Burton-on-Trent*
> *Mar 28th 42*
>
> *Dear Eunice*
>
> *I thought I would send you a few lines to let you know the latest news. I am very upset today to receive the official notice of Eric being posted as <u>missing</u>. It was really the reply to his father's enquiry; so have forwarded it on to Willenhall. There is also another list of local boys all posted as missing same time and place and in some cases same regiment in the 'Mail'. There is only one grain of hope remaining now, as I see it, and that is he may be a prisoner. In this case I fear it will be a long time before any more information is forthcoming.*

> *Enclosed with this communication there is a printed leaflet – Advice to relatives of men reported missing. In this we are warned against listening to enemy broadcasts, also amongst other things it seems the prisoners themselves are allowed to send to relatives a <u>'Captured Card'</u> made out by themselves and this they ask to be forwarded to them if this is the first intimation we have received. So I wonder now if we shall get one of these; if so it should soon be arriving I should think.*
>
> *If <u>only we could know he was safe and being decently treated</u> it would be some comfort, but the suspense and the waiting is dreadful isn't it? Please excuse more now, I shall be glad to know if you have gathered any replies either from Swadlincote or from Mrs Jim Parker.*
>
>
>
> *With much love.*
> *Yours affectionately*
> *L. Degg*
>
>

No 'Captured Card' was ever issued or received. As the notification of 'Missing' was inconclusive, Aunt Lilian continued to hope that Eric may have escaped and would be in touch soon. Bette also received the news that Jim Parker had been posted as 'Missing'. She now realized why Eunice had been so concerned about Singapore.

>
>
> *21 Glasgow Road,*
> *Paisley,*
> *Scotland.*
> *30th March 1942*
>
>
>
> *My dear Eunice,*
> *I really don't know how to begin this letter, I have received very distressing news this morning and needless to say, my heart is very heavy.*
>
> *This morning I was notified that Jim had been reported missing, it says he was serving in Malaya when the garrison of Singapore capitulated on the 15th February 1942. Every endeavour is being made through diplomatic and other channels to obtain information concerning him. It is hoped that he is safe and, although he may be a prisoner of war, it is necessary to post him as 'Missing' pending receipt of some definite information. So don't be at all surprised about Eric also being posted missing, as you know there were thousands of prisoners taken. You were quite right when you dreaded him being sent there.*

> *This has come as a great blow Eunice, and I do pray that they are safe. Do let me know if you have any word from Eric, but as you haven't heard anything further I have my doubts. I hope you will excuse this short note, but I really can't write any more.*
>
> *God Bless You.*
> *Affectionately Yours,*
> *Bette*

As Aunt Lilian had received the official notification that Eric was 'Missing', Eunice wrote once more to the British Red Cross. However, they were unable to provide any further information.

Chapter 9

February–May 1942: Changi, Singapore

We were instructed to go to Changi Barracks which was to the east of the island. On 17 February I collected what could be carried and with what kit we had (we did have two or three trucks), we set out to march the 30 miles to Changi.

There was a fair amount of tinned food at our B Echelon and I put the word around that it would be as well if we took as much food with us as we could. I had acquired a Royal Air Force (RAF) blanket which I was carrying under my arm and at the expense of losing some of my kit I had filled a haversack with tinned food. En route to Changi I put my blanket just behind the tail board of one of the vehicles in front of me but when I arrived at Changi it was missing. Fortunately a man found me an old brown Army blanket which I still had three and a half years later. It was then more like a brown lace curtain and I used it as a mosquito net!

Changi Barracks had been bombed and I think there were still bodies within the rubble – there was the never-forgotten (sweet) smell of decomposing human flesh. When we arrived at Changi we had collected together about 400/500 men. They were told that if they wanted anything for an evening meal they should hand over anything they had brought. My friend George and I emptied our haversacks of tinned food onto the ground; we kept nothing. A few other men emerged and added small quantities to the pile – the men dispersed and the pile was very small. That night a very thin soup was prepared and all had some. Later in the darkness I was aware that men were eating tins of bully beef and other things. I felt very angry and hoped that this attitude was not a precursor of things to come.

All units were called upon to provide nominal rolls, details of casualties and other information. I had continued checking one piece of information against another, until I thought I had accounted for all the men. These records, and others, were buried in a grave marked 'R.E. Cords' or 'Private R.E. Cords'. The burial was in Changi Military Cemetery. Whether or not these records were still there after the war, I have no idea.

Some poor quality rice was obtained from the Japs. I was told by those who knew that this rice had been treated with lime, being intended for seed. We tried to wash the lime, but this was not a success. When cooked it had a very peculiar smell and taste. It also turned a variety of colours. There was very little other food and in about two weeks my friend George White and I were so weak that it took both of us to carry half a bucket of water. The wounded were now being brought together and it was decided that what remained of Changi Barracks should be used as a hospital. This meant that we (those who were fit) had to vacate the area and we moved into a coconut grove. The undergrowth was quite high and we proceeded to cut this down to make a camp. Apart from other creatures there was a great quantity of ants. These appeared to live off the coconut palms and to fertilize them in return. Whilst we were working, the Brigadier of the 55th Brigade appeared and shouted 'Set fire to the undergrowth.' We did this and discovered that the ants went up the trees and later returned when the fires had died down. When things were burning merrily, panic was caused by the discovery of a pit containing a large quantity of howitzer shells.

The brigadier of the 55th Brigade was Tristram Hugh 'Tim' Massy-Beresford, the creator of 'Massy Force', a guerrilla warfare unit formed prior to the capture of Singapore. Brigadier Massy-Beresford was later removed, along with other important captives, to internment at Mukden in China. He was liberated by Soviet forces in 1945 and returned to the UK via the USA.

We had some British Army tents which we erected. Food was still bad and men started to go down with malaria and dysentery. I had an attack of the latter which was most unpleasant. We ate any coconuts which fell from the trees but they did not improve the condition of our internals. I managed to make myself a bed from some timber I found. This had four legs and was covered with a rice bag. However, the ants climbed the legs and became a nuisance. I acquired four bully beef tins, filled them with water and set the four bed legs in them. The outcome of this was that some ants drowned themselves in the water and the others walked across their bodies and up my bed legs. I gave up and was later to discover that ants were a very minor matter compared with other creatures.

After a couple of weeks or so the Japs ordered us to send a working party down to Singapore. I suppose our CO and the Adjutant prepared a list of two or three hundred men to go. The Adjutant (my friendly TA one) appeared from a tent and shouted 'Roberts, you are going down to Singapore.' The other names on the party were then read. Needless to say the Adjutant avoided the working party, as did his few TA cronies. The following day a party (including our CO) marched down to Singapore where we were quartered in Farrar Park. We were provided with British Army tents and it was not a bad site. There was reasonable food and each day we were called upon to provide a number of working parties which went out with one Officer or a Senior NCO and a Jap or two. I first went out in charge of a party to a post office depot, where we were instructed to pack telephone equipment into boxes for shipment to Japan. This went on all day. The Jap Officer with us was quite polite, spoke some English and went off to find food for us at midday. The following day I went with a party to a Ford assembly plant which assembled small trucks from components shipped out from the USA. There I was instructed to build a guard house by the entrance to the factory. A few yards away was an Australian party who had been told to do the same thing. There was quite a bit of confusion and I was glad I didn't return to that job next day.

After a couple of weeks we marched back to Changi but not for long. We were soon called to go once again down to Singapore. Needless to say, the Adjutant (Coxon) and his friends did not go (I heard later it was their idea to keep 1/5 Foresters HQ together but the CO, Lieutenant Colonel Lilly, always went and I suppose I was a member of Battalion HQ). I can only assume that the CO didn't want these men.

Chapter 10

Home Front: August–October 1942

In August 1942 Eunice wrote to the British Red Cross again. By now plans were being made to repatriate some civilians from the Far East. It was anticipated that further information would be released with them, but the Red Cross confirmed in September this did not happen.

With little expectation of any response, Eunice wrote to the prime minister once more and saved a copy of the letter she sent:

> *My Dear Prime Minister*
> *I must be the representative of many thousands of people whose life from day to day, morning to evening, without respite, is shadowed by great anxiety – anxiety which surely need not be endured. It is now nearly eight months since the fall of Singapore, upon which occasion, I am given to understand that 60,000 of our men were taken prisoner by the Japanese. Surely, with so many men reported 'Missing' it would justify the 'cost' of an effort to find out what is happening to them – whether indeed they <u>are</u> prisoners (for we do not even know that) and how they are being treated; lists of names which were supposed to have been sent by the repatriation ships were not on board when the ships reached Lourenco Marques – presumably no one really cares about this, and it is the business of no-one in particular to find out why they were not sent and how and when we may expect to receive them. (I have written to the Red Cross Society regarding the matter, but they can tell me nothing.) There are, I am assured, men in various parts of the Empire who have escaped from Singapore, but how can I get in touch with them to see if they have any tiding to impart? How do we know how our men fare if they fall sick – they may even die by the hundred for lack of medical attention, and who cares about that, but we whose hands are tied so that we are utterly powerless to help; the only thing we can do is lie awake at night and endure the agony that these thoughts are bound to bring. My fiancé is only one of these 60,000 but if all the others mean as much to someone as he does to me I can assure you that if you could investigate the matter for us and obtain the information we so much desire,*

> you would earn the undying gratitude of hosts of relatives and friends who at present can do nothing but watch and wonder and wait, and whose work is impeded by this constant anxiety.
>
> If I cannot appeal to you to alleviate my worry and grief for <u>one</u>, may I not entreat your sympathy on behalf of SIXTY THOUSAND?
>
> I know by heart the usual War Office postcards to the effect that the matter is receiving their attention; I should rest very much easier in my bed if I know that the matter was receiving <u>your</u> personal attention.
>
> Thanking you, I remain, sir
> Your obedient servant
> (signed) Eunice M. Lowe

As Eunice predicted, the reply provided no further assistance, but noted that her letter had been forwarded to the War Office.

> PRIME MINISTER
> 10 Downing Street
> Whitehall
> 17th September 1942
>
> Dear Madam,
> I write on behalf of the Prime Minister to acknowledge the receipt of your letter of the 14th September. While Mr. Churchill has every sympathy with your anxiety for news about prisoners of war from Singapore, he regrets that there is no means whereby he can assist you personally. He is therefore having your letter forwarded to the Prisoners of War Department of the War Office.
> Yours truly,
> J.H. Peck

Information concerning officers continued to be released and appeared in the local and national press. On 24 September an obituary appeared in *The Times* of Lieutenant Robert Hugh Irvine (113410) of the 2nd Battalion, Gordon Highlanders, who was killed in action at Singapore on 13 February 1942. In desperation Eunice contacted Lieutenant Irvine's mother to see if she could learn anything about Eric's fate. Eunice saved a copy of the letter she wrote and the touching and gracious reply she received from Lieutenant Irvine's mother:

> Brook Cottage Farm,
> Over Whitacre,
> Coleshill,
> Nr. Birmingham
> 24 September 1942

Dear Mrs. Irvine,

First of all may I apologise for troubling you at this time and express my sympathy with you upon the loss of your son in Singapore.

My reason for venturing to write to you is because I saw the obituary notice in The Times of to-day's date and wondered if you would mind letting me know through what channels you heard of the death of your son. You see, my fiancé, who belongs to the 1/5 Bn. Sherwood Foresters, arrived in Singapore on 11 February last, and was duly reported Missing after the fall thereof on 15 February. I believe the Gordon Highlanders and Sherwood Foresters were in action together in France, and assume that they went together to Singapore. As you will no doubt presume I have sought by every means within my power to obtain further information, but so far without avail – the only thing I can do is to continue writing to him every week via the Japanese Red Cross, Tokio [sic], presuming that he is a prisoner of war; I have been in communication with our Red Cross Society very recently and received a reply to the effect that no names whatsoever had been supplied so far by the Japanese.

Eric left England round about the 29 October last year, arriving in India (Bombay) approximately 29 December. The last letter I had from him was dated 18 January. My information that he arrived in Singapore on 11 February was supplied by the Medical Officer of Health for Singapore, Dr. Shaw, who left the Island on the 12th. He saw the 18th Division arrive there.

With many thanks in anticipation of your kind reply.

> I am,
> Yours sincerely,
> Eunice M. Lowe

> *Drum Castle,*
> *Drumoak,*
> *Aberdeenshire*
> *25-9-42*
>
> *Dear Miss Lowe,*
> *I am afraid I can be no help over news from Singapore. The way I heard about my son was from the War Office. The news had got to them from an officer of the Gordon Highlanders who was sent off by the Colonel with the regimental records the day before the fall of Singapore. After many adventures he arrived at Ceylon, from where he has sent home the news.*
>
> *My son had been out in Singapore with the 2/Gordons for a year before Japan came into the war. I fancy it was the 1st Battalion which was in France and they are all prisoners in Germany.*
>
> *I saw in the paper that postcards from prisoners at Singapore would be arriving shortly and about the 8 Oct. the first shipload of civilian prisoners from the Far East will arrive in this country. So one may hope to hear something and perhaps there may be lists of prisoners. It is dreadfully hard waiting all these weary months I feel almost lucky to know the worst and not to have any more anxious thoughts about Robert. I wish I could have been more helpful to you and with many thanks for your kind sympathy.*
> *Yours sincerely*
> *Dorothy I.F. Irvine*

In October 1942, Eunice received a reply from the War Office to her letter sent to the prime minister:

The War Office
(Cas. P.W.)
Curzon Street House,
Curzon Street,
London, W.1.

GEN/117 (Cas. P.W.)
4 October 1942

Madam,
   In reply to your letter of 14 September, addressed to the Prime Minister, I am directed to assure you that the anxiety of the relatives of personnel missing in the Far East is most fully appreciated and to state that the delay on the part of the Japanese Authorities in furnishing the names of British personnel taken prisoner in the Far East has been a matter of grave concern to the British Government. Every possible step has been taken through diplomatic and other channels to impress upon the Japanese Government the urgency of the case.
   The Japanese Government have for some time promised to furnish complete lists, but these are still awaited. Strong representations have, however, already been made through the Protecting Power as to the reasons for the non-arrival of these lists and when they may be expected. It must be remembered that the Japanese are not signatories to the International Convention relative to the treatment of prisoners of war, although they have agreed to abide by its terms. Moreover, there are no means, unfortunately, open to the British Government by which the enemy can be forced to give information regarding prisoners of war against their own inclination.
   Any officer or other rank who has escaped from enemy hands must report to his nearest military Headquarters and give any information which he may possess. Any news regarding individuals is forwarded to the next-of-kin of those concerned at once. You may be assured that no source of information has been or will be neglected and that, far from remaining passive as you suggest in your letter, H.M. Government are sparing no effort to obtain news and improve the lot of those who are prisoners of war in the Far East by every means in their power.

I am,
Madam,
Your obedient Servant,
G.T.H. Ropis

In early October a friend of Eunice told her of a man, Sergeant Jobber, in the Queen Elizabeth Hospital who was with the 1/5 Foresters in Singapore and who knew Eric. Eunice wrote to him and asked if he would speak to her.

Eunice wrote in her diary that they chatted for an hour, but unfortunately no further details are recorded. Eunice kept a comprehensive scrapbook that contains many newspaper articles of escapees, casualties and of local men who were captured in the Far East, but even in this there is no mention of Sergeant Jobber. Several notes sent to Eunice from Sergeant Jobber indicate that he was bound by the Official Secrets Act.

> *Message Ward Room 6*
> *Queen Elizabeth Hospital*
> *Birmingham*
> *12 Oct 1942*
>
> *Dear Miss Lowe*
> *Thank you for your letter received this morning; of cause [sic] knowing your remarks are too flattering, I am vain enough to be very pleased. So thank you again for being so sweet. Believe me young lady it's quite a pleasure to answer questions to sensible people because they have something in common to discuss and it pleases me to help, because at the same time I can get off my chest lots of things that the average person doesn't want to know.*
> *I honestly wish they would let me broadcast the whole true story, it would relieve the anxiety of thousands of people, but it seems our Bosses want to give a dirty impression of our enemy and so cause hatred.*
> *That is why you were never told the truth in the first place. They are afraid to admit that it was their fault. Please don't hesitate to write me if anything else crops up. I shall always be delighted to help you. I will close now, I'm afraid of boring you to death. Wishing you all the very best of luck and just reminding you to let me know if <u>you</u> hear anything.*
> *For auntie – I was taken prisoner on the morning of the 16th February 1942 and left Singapore on the last day of the month. Sorry, I can't divulge when I arrived in the UK.*
> *Cheerio*
> *Sergeant R.C. Jobber*

Those who escaped from the Far East were interrogated by the British authorities to gather any intelligence. These records are held at Kew Public Records Office; however, Sergeant Jobber's record was not with the others. A note was left in the file stating that it had been removed. His record has yet to be located.

Chapter 11

May–October 1942: River Valley Road Camp, Singapore

We moved from Singapore and to a camp (River Valley Camp) which had been constructed by the British as a refugee camp. It was a reasonably well-organized place with a number of huts and surrounded by a fence. The huts were constructed from timber and were set around a parade ground. There was an entrance to each hut from the parade ground and for the length of the hut, on either side, was a wooden platform set up about 18" from the ground upon which the men slept. Marching down from Singapore, I decided that I would slip into anonymity as most of the others had done and not always be exposed as seemed to be the case in the past. However, when we marched into River Valley Camp, 150 men were allocated to each hut and I heard the voice of a superior shout 'Right, Roberts, you are in charge of this hut.' I found that several of the men in the hut were senior to me, so I had to assume authority over them.

George White recalled that

> After about 6 weeks when the Japs wanted prisoners in camps in the town Eric, Sergeant Pat Kavanagh (the Royal Army Ordnance Corps member), Lance Corporal Dixon and I ended up in River Valley Road Camp occupying a section of a hut near the door. Under Eric's direction, our small location finally ended up with a small table, two manufactured (by Eric) chairs and four bunk beds, two on each side of the table area. As Eric's duties for the CO in the camp office kept him in the camp all day, he was able to find time to improve our hut space.

Sergeant Patrick Ralph Kavanagh (7612221) came from Cheshire and enlisted in October 1939; he served with the 18th Division. Lance

Corporal Michael George Dixon (4753908) was another 1/5 Forester and came from Enfield in Middlesex. Both men survived the camps and returned home in 1945.

> The Japanese were not really concerned about the Geneva Convention where the treatment of PoWs were concerned but they did agree that commissioned officers would not be 'expected to do manual work'; this applied also to some senior NCOs, and that such would be employed in a supervisory capacity. It followed that an officer or a senior NCO was placed in charge of each hut with 150 men and he was allowed to have an orderly to keep the hut clean and tidy. The Officer in charge was expected to maintain order and discipline, organise work parties when called for by the Japs and supervise the distribution of food. This was my job and I suppose there were other duties too. I was still keeping a record of 1/5 Battalion affairs. Initially things were a bit tricky, there was some fighting amongst the men and there were those who refused to accept my orders, saying they would only take orders from the Japs. In a fairly short time all these problems were overcome.

George White noted that

> River Valley Camp was fairly reasonably run by the Japs. Out of camp work was mainly on building *godowns* (small warehouses) on a patch of land about a mile distant. My memory of it was that we were able to make ourselves reasonably comfortable and had time in the evenings to relax. It was here that Lance Corporal Mike Dixon and I were taught by Eric and Pat to play bridge and between us we carved a chess set and made a board. I remember that I carved the knights and made a very good job of them, according to Eric. What happened to the set after we left River Valley I do not know.

> However, a problem arose concerning boots. The Japs said that if men had no boots they would be excused from working parties on the docks, building sites and other places. After a little while I found that boots were being hidden and less and less men were leaving each day on working parties. I could see that this was leading to trouble

and spoke to the men about it who responded by enquiring if I was working for the Japs. One day we had in our rations some potatoes which were very much like English new potatoes and the following day, after the working party had left the camp, I thought I might see if I could acquire a few of these potatoes from the food store. On the far side of the camp well away from the living huts we had a food store and I went over there to see what I could find. I was in the shade of the hut when the camp gates were opened and into the camp came at the double several dozen Jap soldiers with fixed bayonets, headed by an Officer with drawn sword. I drew back into the shadow of the hut and waited. The Japs proceeded to go through all the huts and drive forth at bayonet point all the men they could find therein. They were assembled on the parade ground and marched out of the camp on some work. When the dust had settled, I emerged and went back to my hut. The following morning, a goodly number of men turned out for work, all with their boots.

Time went on but more and more men were falling sick with a variety of ailments, apart from malaria and dysentery, most were due to malnutrition or the heat. Whilst it is inevitable under such conditions, self-survival was almost paramount but invariably men worked for each other, the fitter ones helped the sick. Generally there was a fair distribution of what was available. Men were buried decently and so far as possible their graves recorded. Some men survived against all the odds, whilst others died who might reasonably have been expected to survive. Whilst I was at River Valley Camp in Singapore, I had a number of men in my hut who had joined the 1/5 Foresters in Norfolk, who were Jews and mainly from the East End of London. Not having much experience of such, I spent some time talking to them and picked up a little Yiddish (which I later found that I would have been better without). Most had Russian and German origins. The more orthodox were inclined to keep together and exclude others. Although we were all living under the same circumstances, for reasons I could not analyse they were not survivors. I cannot bring to mind any of that little group from River Valley Camp who did survive. In 1943, I recollect one man, Kreiger, a burly man, who the Medical Officer (MO) supported in any way he could. He was on the way to recovery when he died. I spoke to the MO about this (by now the MO had much experience of tropical diseases) and he said 'He just gave up.' I suppose other men who were not of Jewish extraction did the same thing.

Private Alfred Kreiger (4750648) was a member of the Motor Transport Section and died of cholera at Tonchan on 12 July 1943. He was buried at the Cholera Cemetery, Grave 91, Tonchan Main Camp Cemetery. He was married and lived at 4 Hartland Court, Friern Barnet Road, London.

In about July 1942, we received a quantity of Red Cross goods. There were some felt hats, sleeveless cloth pullovers, there may have been some boots and also a collection of food items. Bully beef, porridge oats, *atta* and *ghi*. *Atta* is coarsely ground maize and *ghi* is a vegetable fat which was obviously intended for the Indian troops who had been taken prisoner. The Red Cross goods had been sent via Lorenqo Marques [*sic*] in Portuguese East Africa and arrived just before we were told by the Japs that we were to go to a rest camp in Thailand. So, having been issued with the Red Cross stuff and carrying as much as we could, we were loaded into steel railway vans to go north.

George White noted that

Under the illusion fostered by the Japs that we were to be moved to better camps in Malaya – we set out from Singapore in metal rail wagons, overcrowded (about 35 to a wagon), for an unknown destination.

I was one of 500 men identified as B Battalion and the British Officer in charge was Lieutenant Colonel Lilly. Another group of men (A Battalion) had preceded us. Our train proceeded north and we had one stop at Kuala Lumpur where we were given some food at the railway station. This was a very fine Victorian building.

We eventually got off the train at a place called Banpong [*sic*] which was on the Malay/Thai border. [According to George White the journey took about five days.] A transit camp had been built there and this was under a foot or two of water. However, we spent one night there and the following morning we were told that we had several

May–October 1942: River Valley Road Camp, Singapore

days' march ahead of us and if we left some of our heavy baggage it would be sent on for us. I didn't like this but not knowing what was ahead, I took all my kit but left a pack of Red Cross food to be sent on later. The pack was strapped up and marked with my name. Later we set out on quite a good metalled road and at about 1600 hrs stopped at a staging camp where we spent the night. Next day we moved rather a longer distance and spent a night at a place called Kanburi.

George White's recollections differed to Eric's:

Eric refers to our spending a night at a staging camp before arriving at Kanburi. My recollection is that we got to Kanburi in one day and that after we left Kanburi, we stayed a night at Banpong [sic] where there was a Buddhist shrine, then we went on to the 'wide river'. From there began the march to the River Kwai – the first day (about 25 miles) to Kanburi carrying what personal kit we possessed and all the cooking utensils and other stores which could be managed. The four of us managed to complete the march, utterly exhausted on arrival at the river at Kanburi, where parts of tents provided some shelter. The CO defied Jap demands that we march again next day. I should explain that our party was made up mainly of those Foresters who had been fit enough on leaving Changi with a few other ranks from other 55th Brigade battalions.

There I settled down for the night with my head on my kit. When I awoke the contents of my haversack had been stolen – this was a serious loss. Next day we moved along a track which had been cleared through the jungle and spent another night as best we could. Next day the same, and after about eight hours we arrived on the bank of a wide river. We were ferried on boats to the far bank where we were to have some food and spend the night.

We were in the open and there was no cover – at two or three o'clock in the morning heavy monsoon rain fell upon us and everything we had became soaking wet. All were standing around in whatever they had to cover themselves and one man started to light a fire from some dry leaves from under the trees, I joined him and we eventually built the fire up into a fine blaze. Most of the 500 men gathered around the fire but very few helped with the fuelling of it. A few men worked continually and we had difficulty in forcing our way through the circle of men standing around it to put our fuel upon the fire. I was pulling up small bamboos by the roots; we had no axe. On other occasions I tried to pull up the same bamboos by hand but I was never able to achieve it again. [Bamboo burns in both wet and dry states, hence its use as fuel during the monsoons.]

When daylight came, it was agreed with the Japs that our continued journey would be delayed a little so that we could dry ourselves and our belongings. We set out at midday with a Jap leading along jungle tracks. At 1600 hrs we found ourselves back at the point of our departure four hours earlier. We started again and before we reached our destination darkness had fallen. I was very wearied and sank down upon the ground; fortunately a friend of mine missed me and retraced his steps, found me and encouraged me to press on. I went with him and we caught up with the rest of the party and later we arrived at our destination, a clearing in the jungle where some huts made from bamboo and *attap* had been erected by others. [*Attap* is a type of palm used in the construction of huts and houses in Malaysia and Indonesia. The leaves from the tree are used to make a type of thatch.] Once again we settled down for the night. We were not in very good shape; one man had died on the journey from Banpong [*sic*], a Petty Officer from HMS *Repulse* which had been sunk by the Japs.

There were no deaths of Royal Navy personnel in Thailand in late 1942. However, a sub-lieutenant in the Straits Settlement Royal Naval Volunteer Reserve (SSRNVR) died in November 1942 at Ban Pong Transit Camp, Thailand from dysentery and malaria. This was Peter Dickenson, an assistant rubber planter from Malacca. He was born in Sheringham, Norfolk in October 1919 and is buried at Kanchanaburi Cemetery. It seems highly likely that this was the man mentioned here.

It emerged a day or two before that we were to be engaged upon clearing the jungle in preparation for a railway line to be laid between Bangkok and Rangoon. We were now in a place which the Japs had called Wampo. However, immediately prior to our arrival at Wampo we spent one night at Tarsao, where an advance party had erected a number of bamboo huts.

Chapter 12

Home Front: November 1942–May 1943

By November 1942 Eunice was in contact with the British Red Cross and names continued to trickle through, but still no word of Eric. Eunice continued to write a letter each week to Eric c/o the Japanese Red Cross:

> WAR ORGANISATION
> OF THE
> BRITISH RED CROSS SOCIETY and ORDER OF ST JOHN
> PRISONERS OF WAR DEPARTMENT
>
> 27 November 1942
>
> Sergeant E.B. Roberts, 4978071 Sherwood Foresters
>
> Dear Miss Lowe,
> We have had your letter asking if it is possible for you to obtain a Prisoner of War magazine. You can do this by writing to the Prisoners of War Department, St. James's Palace, London, S.W.1 and they will make arrangements for you to have this sent as we do not deal with it in this Department.
> We have had a certain number of names sent us recently by the Japanese though by far the greater number are still to come. It is, however, encouraging that some lists have reached this country and gives us hope that the rest may follow before too long. We will, of course, let you know as soon as there is anything we can tell you about your fiancé as we well realise how anxious you must be.
> It is quite correct to address your letters C/o. the Japanese Red Cross and we hope very much that you may hear in course of time that he has heard from you. This is the only way to write at the present time.
> Yours sincerely,
> p.p. Margaret Ampthill
> Chairman

By the end of December 1942, since the Fall of Singapore in February, Eunice had written thirty-six letters to Eric. She had received no replies but continued to write. Many did the same, but addressed to men who had already died or been killed months before. Beyond the notification of 'Missing' there was no further official information. However, the names of 1/5 officers captured at Singapore began to appear in the local papers.

In January 1943, the first anniversary of the Fall of Singapore was approaching. Eunice had yet to hear any news from or about Eric. She again contacted the War Office and her local MP to appeal for information. Eunice kept copies of the letters she sent, including the appeal to the War Office:

> *Brook Cottage Farm,*
> *Over Whitacre,*
> *Coleshill,*
> *Nr. Birmingham*
> *25th January 1943*
>
> *The War Office*
> *LONDON.*
>
> *Dear Sirs,*
> *Exactly twelve months ago tomorrow my fiancé, together with some fifty-nine thousand, nine hundred and ninety-nine other young men, arrived at Singapore. Apparently you cared little about them then – it would certainly appear that you care less about them now, for at the end of February last year the relatives of all these men were notified that they were 'Missing' and since then 1100 names only have come through from the Japanese as being prisoners of war, and these all names of officers. Is it not high time that drastic steps were taken to obtain particulars as to the whereabouts and treatment of these men, who seem now to have simply disappeared into the blanks of oblivion – or maybe I am just about twelve months or so premature in my suggestions and you would prefer to give the Japanese a little more time to work their diabolical will upon their helpless and hapless victims?*
>
> *I wrote to you some months ago, and was informed upon that occasion that 'all possible steps were being taken' and 'everything possible was being done'. I have waited as patiently as may be, together with all the other relatives of these*

men, multitudes of them, reassured by your letter and confident that news would not be long delayed, but still the weary months go by and Singapore is forgotten as a 'closed chapter', a blot on the fair page of British history, no reference is ever made to the men in Malaya bar the fact that 'nothing at all is known about them <u>at present</u>'. How much longer is this going to go on, and how many more terribly anxious and nerve-wracking years are to go by before we can know even the bare facts of whether they are still in existence or not?

I write to my fiancé every week c/o Japanese Red Cross, but no-one can inform me what becomes of these letters and whether they are ever likely to reach their destination. I suppose they are doomed to the fate of letters written by prisoners of war in the Far East to us – namely just 'put by' until a 'more appropriate moment' arrives for their despatch. I understand, in fact, that no communication of any kind has proceeded either way since the Exchange Ships weighed anchor in July.

If you would indeed take the most urgent and forceful action to find out all that is humanly possible about the men, alleviate their suffering and thus our anxiety, I know I speak for many in saying that we should owe you a deep debt of gratitude.

With many thanks for your kind attention and in anticipation of help and that <u>right early.</u>

<u>*Yours faithfully,*</u>
Miss E.M..Lowe

Eunice received a response several days later from her MP John S.P. Mellor expressing sympathy but that he was unable to assist directly; it was a matter for the War Office. The response from the War Office came in March, which re-stated that lists of captured personnel were still awaited from the Japanese government. There was no information to give.

Having received no word from Eric, Eunice doubted that the letters she sent to the Japanese Red Cross were even being forwarded. She wrote to the Red Cross for some reassurance.

> **WAR ORGANISATION
> OF THE
> BRITISH RED CROSS SOCIETY and ORDER OF ST JOHN
> <u>PRISONERS OF WAR DEPARTMENT</u>**
>
> *12 March 1943*
>
> *When replying please quote reference: FE/A/631*
>
> Dear Miss Lowe,
>
> Thank you for your letter of the 10 March. Until you receive a camp address of your fiancé you should continue addressing your letters c/o Japanese Red Cross, Tokyo, as that Society will, we feel sure, see that when the letters reach them they are forwarded on to the particular camp in which he is located.
>
> Only a small number of prisoners have been moved to the two camps in Korea and we have all details of their names. We have, however, received comparatively few of the names of the prisoners who still remain in Singapore although these are coming in slowly. It is probably that some considerable time will elapse before complete lists are secured, but you may rest assured that immediately any information is received about your fiancé you will at once be notified.
>
> Yours sincerely,
> Controller

At the end of April Eunice wrote her fifty-first letter to Eric, still not knowing if he was dead or alive. Eunice also wrote another letter to the Red Cross; as names were beginning to be released, there was reason to hope for some news.

> *WAR ORGANISATION*
> *OF THE*
> *BRITISH RED CROSS SOCIETY and ORDER OF ST JOHN*
> <u>*PRISONERS OF WAR DEPARTMENT*</u>
>
> *28 April 1943*
>
> *When replying please quote reference: FE/A/631*
>
> *Dear Miss Lowe,*
>
> *In reply to your letter of 25 April, I am able to inform you that lists of prisoners in Japanese hands are being regularly received at the rate of about a thousand names a week. For some weeks the names of those who are in camps in Malaya have been coming through in alphabetical order and we have had a considerable number of names beginning with the letters A, B and C. There are, however, many prisoners in camps in other areas in the Far East who were taken captive in Malaya and lists of their names are also being received without being given any readily discernible order, certainly not in alphabetical sequence. It appears evident that all the Sherwood Foresters are not in camps in Malaya but that some of them may have been transferred to other areas. It is therefore quite impossible to give any accurate idea when the name of your fiancé may come through unless he should still be in a camp in Malaya and the alphabetical sequence in the lists for those camps is maintained. Even then only an estimate can be given of the date but I should say that it may prove to be July or August next.*
>
> *I certainly trust that you will hear earlier than this and that when news does come it will be to say that he is safe and well.*
>
> *Yours sincerely,*
> *Controller*

Eunice, Aunt Lilian and the rest of the family continued to wait.

Chapter 13

October 1942–May 1943: Wampo, Thailand

This may read as a rather bland account of what took place during PoW life but it is now over fifty years on and I suppose the worst events have been pushed into the background. A great deal happened at Wampo. We had no experience of living under such conditions and it took time to adjust.

A typical understatement from Eric: the 18th Division had arrived after a voyage lasting from October 1941 to February 1942. After a brief stop in India they then spent only two weeks on Singapore Island prior to its capture. The men of the division were from the UK and were called up in the first waves of conscription and so included new recruits and part-time Territorials. Between them they had very little experience of life in the Far East. The climate was either scorching sun or gloomy and overcast with monsoon rains. They were not used to the diet or able to distinguish the difference between Asiatic faces. Nor had they any knowledge of cultural traits and concepts such as 'saving face'. The situation in which they found themselves was completely alien to them.

Wampo and other camps were all located by the river which I was informed was the River *me nam kwai noy*, roughly translated as 'large water extra small' [also known as the River Kwai]. The railway track followed the line of the river and without the river we would not have survived. Food was bad, consisting of broken rice, some vegetables when available – these were of a watery type, gourds and similar things. There were also some roots, ginger and yam. Occasionally, dried fish. Apart from rice nothing seemed to be in regular supply. There was no meat, beans or peas.

The rice was poor quality and often contained a quantity of dirt, bugs and droppings from rats and mice. It was impossible to clean the rice as it would take too long and expend too much energy. The vegetables, when supplied, were often rotten. All food was cooked in water, the only source being the river. As water was gathered from the shallows it contained silt, particularly during the monsoons. The results of eating poor quality food cooked in river water were stomach cramps, diarrhoea and dysentery.

> Men who were not sick (there were quite a lot sick) were expected to work and those were paid 10 cents per day. Calculated on the value of the Straits dollar this was equal to 2½d. This was paid out by the Japs in ten-day periods. There was no point in the men having money; there was nowhere it could be spent. So the cash was retained and each man was credited with his earnings, if any. Those who were sick received nothing. Occasionally, Thai or Chinese traders came down the river with eggs, bananas, tomatoes, a rough type of tobacco and palm sugar. [These were invaluable commodities and supplemented the starvation-level rations of the PoWs. The eggs were usually small duck eggs; bananas were also small and sweet. Palm sugar was traded in 'cakes'.] By arrangement with the Japs, using the men's money we bought what we could in bulk. These items were distributed to the men and their accounts charged with the value of the items they had. I suppose it worked well. Another item sold by the traders was sausages made from iguana and pork fat. They were smoked and, provided they were kept dry, remained edible. There were flies everywhere and they settled on all things but I never remember a fly on an iguana sausage; we fried these in whatever oil or fat we could get.

George White recalled that

> I was engaged in distributing eggs, tobacco bundles and other goods which the CO was able to obtain from Thai traders who came up river from Bangkok. In the camp conditions were fairly reasonable as the Camp Commandant, a Lieutenant Hattari, had been to Europe and worked well with Lieutenant Colonel Lilly. Two other labour parties occupied huts here – D Battalion (mainly Straits Settlement Volunteers) and F Battalion (Royal Artillery). But inevitably the rice diet was lowering PoWs health and deaths began to occur. I remember particularly that Eric somehow obtained a few

bags of 'rice-polishings' – rice husks ground to powder – and gave me one with instructions to eat a spoonful a day. This, I believe, helped to cure some jungle ulcers on my legs which had started up. He also devised a way of adapting our webbing equipment to carry what few packs and haversacks we still possessed.

The season consisted of six months' monsoon and six months' dry weather. So far as we could calculate, when the monsoon started, the river could rise 30 feet in a night and it brought down fallen trees, dead animals and other things. Our huts were always built above the high water mark but conditions became very wet and muddy. It was possible to anticipate the time the rain would commence each day. [Monsoon conditions meant that it either rained or was overcast, and this constant gloom would have only added to the alienation and misery of the PoWs.]

In this camp we had two MOs, one from the Royal Army Medical Corps and the other from the Straits Settlement Volunteer Force (SSVF). The latter came from Singapore, having a French mother and a Spanish father; his name was Stanley Septimus Pavillard. [S.S. Pavillard wrote *Bamboo Doctor* which contains vivid accounts of the camps, particularly the impact of cholera at Tonchan.] I think he had his medical training in England for I remember him saying that he had worked in a hospital in Liverpool. We were very short of drugs. S.S. Pavillard seemed to be terrified of falling ill himself and conserved what drugs he had – he slept on them.

With us at this time were a number of men, those who had lived in Malaya and Singapore for some time and were members of the local volunteer forces, SSVF and the Federated Malay States Volunteer Force (FMSVF). It was discovered that some of these men still had a fair amount of cash in Straits dollars and also that through the Thai and Chinese traders on the river we could obtain medicines – for this we needed cash. So IOUs were given to the men with the cash and medicines were obtained. I have no idea whether or not the IOUs were honoured at the end of the war. I suppose quite a few of the men had died. I found that members of the SSVF and FMSVF were an interesting lot, some with a long family history of service in the colonies and I learnt much from conversation with them. There were those who spoke Malay, Thai and some who had studied Mandarin Chinese. Also, being familiar with that part of the world, they were able to identify matters both animal and vegetable which might concern us. [These men were better able to survive in East Asia. They were familiar with all the aspects of life and culture of which men from the UK had no concept. As volunteers they were often professional men and had a wide variety of specialist knowledge.] It was certainly a learning process for me but I was able to make my little contribution in various ways.

More huts were built from bamboo and *attap*. [The huts were bamboo structures with *attap* (dried palm leaves) roofs. The materials provided were insufficient and therefore restricted the size of the huts. The *attap* thatch was also insufficient, with leaking roofs common. There were limited numbers of tools and those which were provided were blunt, rusty or in poor condition. The floors were earth and during the monsoons these would turn to mud.] The total in the camp rose to about 1000 men but there was a lot of sickness, malaria, amoebic dysentery, bacillary dysentery, unknown fevers which we called dengue, tropical ulcers which could be very bad and crippling, scabies, impetigo, jaundice and a variety of other skin diseases. Also the many diseases due to malnutrition. Quite early on there were two cases of peritonitis – there was no choice but to operate but both died. Initially at Wampo, one or two men were dying each day but in the process of time deaths became less.

At the height of railway construction no time was allowed for bathing. Clothes had become an encumbrance, being completely sodden or resulting in chafing and being uncomfortable or unnecessary to wear in the heat. During work, nicks, scratches and cuts rapidly became infected and often resulted in tropical ulcers. Boots also rotted and no replacements were provided. Men were forced from camp to camp and out on working parties with bare feet.

Most men in the camps suffered from a number of ailments caused by lack of sanitation, poor diet and exhaustion. Sick men were not paid (they did not work), and were usually given half-rations. Housley (1995) provides a list of diseases affecting the PoWs at this time. In addition to the ones Eric listed above there were also abscesses, avitaminosis (vitamin deficiency), beriberi (vitamin B1 deficiency), cholera, diarrhoea, diphtheria, diphtheritic scrotums (infected ulcers on the scrotum), gastro-intestinal disorders, pellagra (lack of vitamin B3 resulting in skin inflammation, diarrhoea and mouth sores), pharyngeal paralysis (paralysis of the upper throat), scrotal dermatitis (B2 deficiency), tinea (fungal skin infections), tropical typhus, weeping dermatitis and weeping tinea. Beriberi was common; the initial symptoms included muscle pains and swollen legs, and without treatment the heart eventually failed.

Each day men worked north and south of the camp on clearing the jungle for the railway track, at the same time track levels had to be achieved by building earth embankments and levelling higher stretches.

George White noted that

> Here, parties of prisoners were sent out each day to clear a path through the jungle for the railway and to blast a way through rock at South Wampo. There were unpleasant incidents and casualties caused by the actions of the Jap engineers. Eric would have known a lot about these as he was engaged with camp office duties and frequently had to liaise with the Jap sergeant in charge of the PoWs in camp, a Sergeant Tukeda, and his clerk Nanamura.

The tools used were very poor. There was no mechanical equipment of any sort. Drilling in rock for the placing of explosives all had to be done by hand. Some elephants with their drivers were brought in to haul timber. Also, some Chinese were brought in to saw timbers for bridge work. This was a very laborious job being carried out with large bow saws. Telephone poles and lines were erected along the cleared track. South of Wampo, a trestle bridge was built; this clung to a cliff face and was almost semi-circular in plan. There were Jap prisoner guards (a lot of these were Koreans with Jap NCOs and officers) and Jap engineers who supervised the railway work. Men were beaten by the Japs without cause and the Japs seemed to enjoy this process, not knowing when to call a halt, even for the most trivial or imagined things.

During this time other men, some Dutch from the Dutch East Indies, men from French Indochina (natives, no Frenchmen), also more of our own men from Singapore, all came tramping through heading north to continue the railway work. We did what we could to provide accommodation and some food. Quite a few died en route. So far as I can remember, after a time, one group of about 2000 men came up from Singapore, a lot of whom were in a poor state of health before they started; this was known as F Force and they were heading for Burma.

Eric would have seen F Force pass by the camp at Tonchan in mid-1943 rather than Wampo. By then, the need for more workers was so great that new units were created from the remaining PoWs at Changi, including F Force. The Japanese needed 7,000, but there were insufficient fit men so unfit and sick men were included. They were sent to the northern end of the railway where resources were scarce and inaccessible to traders. Forced to work shifts from 0530 to 0230 hrs the following morning, 44 per cent did not survive. Once the railway was completed one witness who saw their condition described it as 'pitiable', with the men suffering from severe attacks of beriberi, malaria and tropical ulcers. The weight loss per individual averaged around 70lb (31.75kg) and following liberation 80 per cent had to be admitted to hospital immediately (Russell, 1958).

Occasionally we were given a day off from working on the railway; probably the Japs needed a rest and on one or two occasions we put on a little entertainment. One event was the 'White Horse Inn', which was a riot. How on earth costumes were obtained I will never know, neither did I know how blonde wigs were made for the men who were taking women's parts. All in all we had some very clever fellows and there was a great variety of skills. On another occasion we had a quiz. A few religious services were held by a member of the Royal Army Chaplaincy Department (RACD) who happened to be in the camp. Once a Jewish rabbi volunteered to conduct a simple Christian service.

We were given a rest for Christmas Day 1942. There was no meat in our rations and as a special treat a Jap Sergeant of the guard said we would have a pig for Christmas. The Jap Sergeant drew an oval shape with a stick on the dusty ground, representing a pig – he then put a line through it, pointing to one half and saying 'prisoners' and to the other half saying 'Nippon'. There was a Jap guard of about eighty and there would be about 1000 PoWs. Our CO (Lieutenant Colonel Lilly) who was there at the time took the stick from the Jap Sergeant, put a tail on the pig, wiped out the centre dividing line, pointing to the whole of the pig saying 'prisoners' and to the tail saying 'Nippon'. [This incident was recreated in the 1957 film *The Bridge on the River Kwai*.] When the pig arrived it was one of the usual Asian ones about the size of a smallish dog. Word went out that we were to have pork for Christmas but the cooks had a problem. They cut up the pork they had been given into small cubes (about the size of a dice), made some dumplings from yam flour and with a few vegetables they had, made a very thin stew. This was served out and no one had more than one cube of meat. A mighty howl went up from the men who felt that they had been done down and blamed the cooks.

Although I didn't have one, it was obvious that some men had books of a sort and so it was decided to form a library, the entry fee being a book. Fortunately I was given a book by a well-wisher and this consisted of a number of short articles which I found quite interesting. There was an item entitled 'The Life Cycle of an Earthworm', 'A Grain of Sand', 'Life of the South American Bembex' and a number of others. I duly presented this for membership of the library and it was not very well received, but I held my ground, saying that membership was based on a book and that was a book. However, there were other books by Somerset Maugham, John Galsworthy, Geoffrey Farjeon and others, all of which I found acceptable. The Jap Interpreter hearing of our library said he wished to censor the books. In peacetime he had worked in Malaya for the Canada Sun Life Assurance Co. To avoid trouble, the books were duly collected and delivered to the Interpreter. After a time he returned them marked with his stamp and a proviso that the men should not be allowed to read works by Guy de Maupassant, as such books would inflame them. I later discovered that when the books were being taken to the Interpreter, one was dropped, I presume accidentally. I found the remains of this book lying on the ground; all that was left

Eunice Martha Lowe in 1939.

Lance Corporal Eric Bruce Roberts in 1940.

Sergeant E.B. Roberts, Ahmednagar, India, January 1942. The watch was later 'confiscated' by Japanese forces in Singapore.

George White noted that the photographs in India and Singapore were taken using his camera. Fearing what the Japanese response would be if they found a camera in his possession, he gave it to Lance Corporal Michael Dixon. Somehow Lance Corporal Dixon managed to hide the camera through the years in captivity. After the war he gave the developed photographs to George White.

1/5 Foresters Intelligence Section, Ahmednagar, India, January 1942. From left to right: Private J. Daley, Corporal G.W.C. White, Private E. Virgo, Sergeant H. Gregory, Lance Corporal M.G. Dixon, Corporal D. Henderson, Private G. Taft, Private G. Whiting.

All the men photographed here survived. Private J. Daley (4974313) was married and came from Ripley, Derbyshire; he survived the camp at Nong Pladuk, Japan. Corporal George W.C. White (4756254) was married and came from Middlesex. Private E. Virgo (4756222) was married and came from Bristol. Sergeant H. Gregory (4619758) came from London. Lance Corporal M.G. Dixon (4753908) came from Enfield in Middlesex. Lance Corporal D. Henderson (4750693) was another Londoner. Private G. Taft (4978415) from Chilwell, Nottinghamshire survived the camp at Nong Pladuk, Japan. Private G. Whiting (4976737) came from Burton-on-Trent.

Ahmednagar, India, January 1942. From left to right standing: Sergeant H. Gregory, Private J. Daley, Private E. Virgo, unknown, unknown, Sergeant E.B. Roberts. Sitting: unknown, Lance Corporal M.G. Dixon.

Corporal G.W.C. White paying off the bullock cart drivers at Ahmednagar, India, January 1942.

Chinese school/mission at Singapore, February 1942. The 1/5th Battalion HQ Company was quartered here for the night on arriving at Singapore.

Unknown locations, Singapore, February 1942.

Wedding photo of Jim and Bette Parker, 1940, in their Salvation Army uniforms.

Corporal George W.C. White, Port Said, 1945.

Eric and Eunice's wedding, 1946. Eric's natural parents, Frank and Dorothy, stand behind him. Eunice's father Henry is on the extreme right. Eric's pre-war friend from his YMCA days, Doug Green, was the best man.

Soldier's service and pay book, as carried by Eric throughout the war.

Eric's unworn service medals: 1939–45 Star, Pacific Star and War Medal, with packets, box and transmission slip.

was a small circular piece of the hard cover, the rest had been eaten by termites. On the piece remaining, I identified the title of the book which was *Calculus Made Easy*.

On the opposite side of the hut where I slept were two men of my Battalion – they were friends. Early one morning, I heard one say to the other (he spoke in a very broad Nottingham accent) 'Look 'ere, Oscar, I am about fed o' thee, come outside and take thee shirt off.' They had no shirts on – just a piece of rag around their vitals. Above one man's bed space had been hung a bunch of bananas and in order to defeat the rats he had tied them suspended on a bootlace to the roof. All that now remained of them were the skins covered with bat claw marks. He thought his friend had eaten them and so we watched whilst they went outside and gave each other a couple of thumps, before explaining to them the activities of fruit bats. To guard against bats it was normal to wrap bananas in a cloth of some sort as well as hanging them up.

One night we had a party from French Indochina staying in the camp – they were on their way north. Someone started to sing *Jerusalem*. In the camp at that time, apart from English, French and Dutch were also spoken and they all seemed to join in with great enthusiasm. The Jap guard of eighty men was terrified and ran away into the jungle. The following day, the Japs told us never to sing again.

Unfortunately, beatings by the Japs and their Korean stooges were not uncommon. They seemed to enjoy inflicting injury on those who could not fight back. They were even brutal to each other. I remember a case at Wampo where something upset a visiting Jap officer who proceeded to beat a Jap warrant officer standing nearby; he in his turn beat a Jap of lower rank who proceeded to beat up a Jap private soldier, who in his turn took it out of some prisoners who were nearby. The whole business was a nonsense but, as proved at the end of the war when the tables were turned, the Japs were a craven lot.

At Wampo, apart from malaria, I caught impetigo. Many men grew beards and I followed suit, then came the impetigo. The MO told me what my problem was and told me to shave, saying some ointment would be provided by the Medical Corporal. I shaved and went to the Corporal who said he hadn't any ointment. However, he said if he had some petroleum jelly he could make some up. I had a tin of anti-mosquito ointment and offered this as a base. He took this and I had one treatment from it. The next day when I went for a further dose, he said he hadn't anything. I am afraid I took him roughly, saying he had already had my ointment. This was produced and I had several more treatments but I think the problem was mainly cured by regular bathing with near-boiling water.

Irrespective of how clean we tried to keep ourselves, we all had body lice. Lice eggs were laid in the seams of clothing and seemed to be quite immune to being boiled. Bugs infested our bedding but bugs could not tolerate sunlight, so our bedding was put out in the hot sun away from where we were sleeping. The bugs went under the bedding to protect themselves from the sun and we then snatched the bedding away to leave them to die. This was a continual battle but some men didn't care and I think it was from them that those who were more vigilant were re-infested. [The huts were also infested with biting insects. This was in addition to the mosquitoes which proliferated following the monsoon rains.]

Many men had scabies. This was a particularly unpleasant thing. Scabies are small insects rather like a flea which burrow into the skin; a pupal chamber is created, eggs are laid and hatch out. The young scabies then proceed under the skin in all directions and repeat the process. I believe sulphur baths are the treatment for this problem but nothing was available to us and septic sores developed, particularly on the backside. I suffered in this way and developed an abscess – I couldn't sit down without discomfort. I went to the MO who almost gleefully announced that I had a large abscess and if I came back later in the day he would cut it out. I knew that in order to do this he usually borrowed an open razor. I was not keen to have this done and asked my friend George White if he would bathe the abscess for me. He did this over a week or two with near-boiling water. The abscess was dispersed and the scabies attack came to an end.

We were never free from rats and they came at night and nibbled away at the hard skin on our feet, awakening us when they drew blood. There were very large centipedes, the length of a man's finger. They didn't sting but if they crawled onto a person and were knocked off in the wrong direction, they would dig their feet in and very painful scratches resulted. I can confirm that a centipede has thirty-two pairs of legs (sixty-four in all) and not one hundred as their name suggests. There were scorpions, most quite small but I came across one which was the size of a small crayfish. I wasn't believed when I mentioned this to others but later I was to discover written evidence of this large species.

In the jungle there were snakes of various sorts including constrictors and although we saw evidence of snakes, we were generally not troubled by them. Monkeys and apes could usually be heard but not often seen; although I was told that in some places they were quite a nuisance. Larger animals were present but usually kept clear of the camps. I suppose due to our ignorance we were never able to find anything edible in the jungle apart from bamboo shoots, but I never had any of these. No local people were living in any of the areas we operated in and there was little evidence that this had ever been so.

At Wampo, Lieutenant Colonel Lilly and a group of Officers met for the purpose of recording Japanese atrocities, so far as they were known to them at the date of their meeting. I was given this information and on the portable typewriter belonging to Company Quarter Master Sergeant Nicklin. [Company Quarter Master Sergeant C.F. Nicklin (4976632) was a Derbyshire man and was a close friend of the adjutant, Coxon. He survived and returned home in 1945.] I typed a number of copies which were given to certain officers in the hope that the evidence might survive until the end of the war. I had a copy of this report and this was a very tricky thing to have in one's kit, but I carried it for some time until we arrived at Tamuan in 1944.

Chapter 14

May–August 1943: Tonchan Main Camp and Tonchan Spring Camp, Thailand

Tonchan Main Camp

From Wampo we moved north to an established camp named Tonchan. By now a lot of men were suffering from tropical ulcers on their legs and ankles. This was a progressive thing for which no cure seemed to be available. Many men were sent down river to Nakom Paton (a base hospital) and I gather that up to two amputations a day were carried out there. I was told that most of such surgical work was carried out by an Anglo-Indian who was a warrant officer in the Indian Army Medical Corps. So far as I know, even under those circumstances, it was possible for a man to be moving around within a fortnight with the help of crutches.

I developed an ulcer on my left leg and following the usual pattern, despite the treatment available it became steadily worse. It was very painful and I could only move around by hopping on one foot, using a bamboo pole. The view was that failure for the wound to heal was due to deficiency in our diet, a lack of Vitamin B. Our food consisted mainly of broken grain rice from which the husk had been removed (known as polished rice). The husks appear normally to have been fed to pigs and other animals. Vitamin B being in the rice husks, it was decided that we must try to get some. By arrangement with a boatman, a sack of rice husks was brought up river to us. Efforts were made to get men to eat them by adding them to their food. They were very unpalatable, as they contained rat droppings (as did our rice normally) and large living white grubs. I got some of the rice polishings and proceeded to eat them on a daily basis. I removed the rat droppings so far as I could and to remove the grubs, I held a spoonful of the rice polishings over a mug of near boiling water. The grubs wriggled to the surface and I threw them out, then eating the polishings as they were. After a week or two, much to my relief, I saw that my ulcer was healing and I was soon able to move around normally. So far as I know most of the other men couldn't tolerate eating the rice polishings and they continued to be sent down river. The camp we were in at the time had very sandy soil, probably being the bed of the river when it was very much larger. There were a lot of sand flies which bit my legs and the little punctures they left were not inclined to heal. I was convinced that my ulceration was started by a sand fly bite and pointed this out to the MO with a view to getting men to cover their legs. The MO ridiculed me. However, I covered my legs and had no more ulcers. Later, during the voyage home on HMS *Chitral*, I found a medical book in the library in which it said that sand fly bites could initiate ulcers.

Whilst I had suffered from a type of dysentery early on, I managed to avoid further attacks, mainly due to scrupulously sterilizing everything I used for eating. Never allowing food to remain uncovered; never drinking anything which had not been boiled. Making sure that all food had been well cooked. If I knew this was not the case, I went without the food or drink, but only on one occasion did I knowingly fail. This was an occasion when I foolishly allowed myself to have nothing in my water bottle. It was at the latter part of the rainy season and I dipped my bottle in the water of a paddy field. Having done it I was very worried but survived. When we were on the move, we tried to set off with a water bottle full of either water or tea. The important thing was never to have it empty but always leave some in the bottle. It was the only way to survive.

I have, perhaps, mentioned these matters elsewhere but the men suffered from a great variety of illnesses. Those related to malnutrition (that is directly) such as beriberi (lack of Vitamin B), pellagra (lack of Vitamin A) and others which could not be identified at the time. Then, of course, malaria was prevalent – this took various forms, the early onset when victims would recover and if they remained free of it for about a month, it was said that any further attack was a re-infestation. If the trouble re-occurred in less time it was regarded as recurrent but even then it might clear up. However, in some cases it continued to return and was regarded as chronic. Many people died of this version. There was cholera, typhus, Weil's disease (both the latter I believe carried in the urine of rats). It was difficult under our circumstances to diagnose the diseases, the onset of many being the symptoms of a common cold. So, many people died, probably from a combination of several things. At one stage we had a reasonable amount of quinine and took this as a preventive but I don't think it had much effect. There were a number of skin diseases and also problems with regard to lack of salt. I discovered this early on and made sure I always had salt [rock salt could be obtained from the Thai traders and it was a precious commodity].

A few men remained remarkably free from illness and I recollect one strong young man in this category. He had survived for two and a half years in the jungle without even having malaria. Then malaria struck and he died, just one attack. I imagine everyone had malaria at some time, in varying degrees, but in many cases, after a series of attacks, they became so enfeebled that they died.

To be sent down river to Nakom Paton (referred to as a base hospital) was to me a sentence of death. For one thing, men left their friends and joined a miscellaneous collection of men who were all in the same position. Conditions may have been better there, being nearer areas of settlement. Jim Parker became very ill and was sent down river from Tonchan; I went down to the river to see him off on a boat. I thought I would never see him again but he was one of those who survived [according to Housley (1995), Jim Parker was evacuated from Petchburi on 2 September 1942].

At one stage, the senior Jap in the guard was a warrant officer. He was a large man for a Jap and was known as 'the Tiger'. One day we heard that he planned to go down country for a couple of days and we saw him leave the camp and go towards the river. When he had gone the Japs took off the guard and all congregated in their hut. Then unknown to the Jap guard, 'the Tiger' returned and went to the Guards' Quarters where he found them all. 'The Tiger', picking up a chair, belaboured them all about the head and shoulders with it and drove them to the end of their hut. After a while the guards returned to their duties.

'The Tiger' was Sergeant Watanabe. After the war, Watanabe was sentenced by the War Crimes Trials for a token one day of imprisonment.

It was recognized that he did not go beyond the acceptable limits of treatment which prevailed on the railway and, although severely restricted, did what he could to improve the conditions of the prisoners.

Tonchan Spring Camp

> There was a very wonderful spring of fresh water on the site, which had its origins in the rocks which overshadowed the site. There were also numerous land crabs. For shelter we had a number of old British Army tents. An army tent usually has an inner and an outer canvas, essential under tropical conditions. In our case we had one canvas only, the inner or the outer. Under monsoon conditions the canvas became soaked and the water ran down the inner surface. We dug drainage ditches around the tents in an effort to keep a dry area within. With the rains our camp became a bog. Blasting was taking place in the rocks above and from time to time the camp was showered with falling rocks. Fortunately no one was injured at this camp.

George White added that

> The accommodation was *attap* huts and some tents, we four obtained a tent outer and made ourselves as comfortable as we could (not exactly the right word) by creating beds from poles, signal wire, etc. under the tent outer. It was rather flimsy, but withstood the numerous tropical downpours and gave us space instead of the crowding in the *attap* huts.

Denys Peek was present at the same camp and recalled that these tents were rotten and stank of mildew. Having only an inner or outer cover meant that the tents were flimsy and insufficient for the number of men who needed shelter. With the monsoons those on the edges of the tents were soaked. The Japanese also refused to allow the PoWs any materials for latrines. As these were not roofed they overflowed during the monsoons, adding to the potential for disease, particularly cholera (Peek, 2004).

When we had been in this camp two or three weeks, about 1000 labourers arrived. They seemed to have been forced by the Japanese to work on the railway. [These men were Tamils who were previously workers on rubber plantations in Malaya. Following the Japanese invasion rubber production halted and these men had no work. They were given promises of lucrative wages if they agreed to work on the railway in Siam, but the pay never materialized.] Unlike the PoWs, they had no organisation of their own. In our case we had the vestiges of discipline but they had nothing. Unfortunately, they brought cholera with them and our spring of pure water was contaminated. The labourers suffered badly from cholera, and a large pit was dug for the bodies of those who had died. I fear that in their panic some of the labourers who were thrown into the pit were not already dead. I heard moaning when I walked by the pit. There was nothing to be done. Then one of our men contracted cholera. We had no medicines and I recollect the MO gave the patient potassium permanganate crystals wrapped in rice paper. He was dead in a couple of days and by then the Japs were in a panic. They insisted on our burning the body. It was during the monsoon period and we asked the Japs for petrol or paraffin. We were given about a pint of paraffin for the job. A pyre was built and several men worked throughout the night to burn the body. It was quite a job and examination of the ashes the following day revealed a piece of a shin bone. A number of men died from cholera and I only remember one who survived. Men would go out to work on the railway in the morning, probably returning sick at midday – the following day they were dead. It was a very demoralizing experience; no one knew who would be the next victim. The camp site was very rocky and we had been unable to dig our latrines to the required depth so that the normal chemical process could take place. The latrines were full of maggots and there were clouds of flies. I began to plot the tents in which men had died and found that all of those were within the smell of the latrine. Further, I discovered that in the main, the area of operation of the flies was within the zone of the smell. I was relieved to discover that my tent was outside the vital area.

May–August 1943: Tonchan Main Camp

George White added that

> Spring Camp was, however, a bad camp; malaria attacked all of us. The food was rice with the occasional addition of some sort of vegetable and at times some meat from the one or two buffaloes brought to the camp and butchered, with Jap permission, by our own regimental butcher. Of course the Japs, or rather Koreans as our guards now were, took most of the meat. The working parties were badly treated by the engineers with their '*speedo, speedo*' demands to clear the jungle for the railway track and to this was added the outbreaks of cholera all along the river. At Tonchan we lost a few men, but the outbreak was largely contained in our camp thanks to our doctor, Captain Richardson and medical staff with us. The worst part of this time was the knowledge and sight of many Tamils (forced up the river for forced labour) succumbing to the disease and in many cases being left where they fell. [Captain John Richardson (118168) of the Royal Army Medical Corps was born in 1914 and came from Cambuslang, Scotland. He survived and was repatriated in 1945.]

Generally we moved from camp to camp on foot along animal tracks or perhaps along the track prepared for the railway. However, on one occasion during the monsoon period, we moved by boat on the river. [These were local barges. Men were crammed into them with standing room only. Journeys could last hours or days.] The water was high and we came to a rocky cataract down which a mass of water tumbled. A sea-going tug had been brought up river and was stationed at the head of the cataract. During the dry season it would have been impossible for a boat to get up the cataract but in our case, a rope was attached to the tug above and we were winched up. A man was posted on our boat where the rope was attached. He had an axe and he was ordered to cut the rope if too much water was being taken on board. Under these conditions the prow of our boat dug into the water and we shipped quite a fair amount. At this stage the rope was cut and we went bouncing down the cataract doing our best to fend off the rocks. The tow rope was re-attached and the next attempt was successful.

Chapter 15

Home Front: May 1943–March 1944

In late May 1943, fifteen months after the Fall of Singapore, Eric was confirmed as a prisoner of war in Japanese hands:

> 62 Eton Rd.
> Burton on Trent
> 26 May 1943
>
> Dear Eunice,
>   I expect you will have by now received my wire with the glad news of Eric, and like me you will be feeling <u>somewhat scattered</u>. I had cut out the enclosed from last night's 'Mail' and remarked to Aunty Rose that now the 'M's had been reached we should expect very soon the 'P's and 'R's and wondered how long J. Parker's name would be coming out of the hat.
>   This morning as usual I was watching the postman and thinking I really <u>needn't</u> for I couldn't expect anything today when lo! He turned in our gate and delivered one letter. I picked it up and seeing the War Office on the outside of the envelope was at once stricken with the <u>palsy</u>. As you may imagine I had to first seek my chair and summon all my courage before I dare open it. However, thinking I <u>must</u> use common sense I took the plunge and found the usual office notification to the effect that No. 497807 Sergeant Eric Bruce Roberts is a prisoner of war in Japanese hands, interred Malai Camp. Should any information be received concerning him such information will at once be communicated to us. Also instructions as to the method of communicating with prisoners of war can be obtained at any post office, also a slip that general enquiries about PoWs and of the treatment to which they are entitled may be made in person or by letter at the PoW enquiry centre, Curzon St. House, Curzon St. London W1.
>   I think I have told you all the official news. I think as this was really addressed to Eric's father I had better first send it for their perusal. But later on you may see the document. However, it is of little importance, you will be familiar with the style and brevity of it and the chief concern is to know that at

> *long last we do know something definite and have now only to hope and pray for <u>Eric's safety and speedy return.</u>*
>
> <u>*Congratulations*</u> *to both of us. Well really I must now get on with my neglected duties. Cheerio! And don't go quite through the ceiling.*
>
> *Lots of love from*
> *Aunty Lily*
>
>
> *P.S. I wonder if J. Parker has turned up? I expect he has.*

Bette was also notified that Jim Parker had been captured and wrote to tell Eunice. Most friends and relatives were relieved that their loved ones were prisoners and not dead. They hoped for fair treatment. Eunice wrote to tell Danny O'Brien the news. Danny was by then serving in North Africa.

> *Dear Eunice,*
>
> *A recent letter of my mother gave me the very welcome news that Eric and Jim are alive. God knows it certainly was a long time coming but as I know too well it was very welcome both to you, Eric and Jim's relations. Now we must endeavour to see that their stay in Jap hands ends quickly. I am more than convinced that we are now on the offensive especially now that the Axis are out of North Africa and that Italy is getting softened. I hope it is softened to a jelly.*
>
> *Have been out here three months and it's not so bad. The weather was trying at first but we are used to that. The chief pests are mosquitoes and flies. Whilst we lose one way we gain another. For instance lemons are plentiful here and so we have real lemon juice sans sugar.*
>
> *One of my pals has just heard the news which contained a reference to the list issued by the Japs of prisoners taken in Singapore. All I pray is that the lads are treated in the same manner as the Germans and others are treated here by the Allies. Give my best wishes to Mr and Mrs Roberts and Eric's Aunt and tell them how pleased I am to hear the news.*
>
> *Best wishes*
> *Danny*
>

Finally, word from Eric was received in late August 1943. By this time Eunice had written sixty-eight letters with no response. Eunice wrote in her diary on 21 August 1941: 'Went to Aunty Lily's for tea and found she had received a postcard from Eric so there was great rejoicing.'

Although it was received in August 1943, it was written by Eric more than six months earlier in late 1942. Now Eunice was in a position to share the information with the Red Cross and to ask them for further guidance.

> **WAR ORGANISATION**
> **OF THE**
> **BRITISH RED CROSS SOCIETY and ORDER OF ST JOHN**
> **PRISONERS OF WAR DEPARTMENT**
>
> 17.9.1943
>
> *When replying please quote reference: FE/50186*
> *Sergeant E.B. Roberts*
> *1/5th Sherwood Foresters*
>
> *Dear Miss Lowe*
> *Thank you for your letter advising us that you have received intimation that the above is a prisoner of war in Japanese hands. We are very glad that this news of his safety has at last been received.*
> *Letters and postcards, which must be limited to 25 words not including addresses, may be sent post free to the prisoner. They should be posted in the ordinary way, and not sent to us for onward transmission. Letters should preferably be typewritten, or alternatively they must be written in block capitals. Only relatives and close friends should write, and in present circumstances no object will be served by any one family writing more than once a fortnight. The name and address of the sender must be written on the back of the envelope. (Members of H.M. Forces should give a civilian address of a relative or friend who would be willing to forward replies.) No enclosures whatever, even photographs, are allowed, nor may homemade envelopes or economy labels be used. No reference to Naval, Military, Aerial, Economic or Political matters is permitted.*
> *Your attention is also drawn to the attached leaflet giving particulars of the facilities that we are able to offer for the typing of letters. You will find at the end of this letter the exact method of address that you should use when writing to your prisoner.*
> *Parcels cannot at present be sent owing to the refusal of the Japanese to grant safe conduct for the ships that would have to be utilized for such a parcels*

> service. Every endeavour is being made to secure a change in their present attitude and if, as a result of these efforts, facilities are accorded, the next-of-kin will be advised. Full details will also be published in the Press.
>
> This Organisation, in collaboration with other national Red Cross Societies, is meanwhile doing everything possible to help Far East prisoners by providing food, medicines, clothing and other supplies. Already several thousand tons of such supplies have been shipped to the Far East, and distributed equally among all prisoners of Allied nationality in Japanese hands. Plans have been made, and continue to be made, for the supplementing of these supplies by further despatches and by local purchases in the Far East.
>
> We should like you to know that we shall retain complete records of the prisoner at this office, and shall be only too pleased to render you all assistance. If you write or call please be sure to quote the reference at the head of this letter, as this will enable us to give you prompt attention.
>
> Yours sincerely,
Wkc
for Controller
>
> Letters should be addressed as follows –
> PRISONERS OF WAR POST
> SERVICE DES PRISONNIER DE GUERRE
> 49780741 SERGEANT E.B. ROBERTS
> BRITISH PRISONER OF WAR
> MALAYA CAMPS (Malai and Malaya are the same but we advise the above form of spelling to be used)

In late 1943 Eunice learned that Eric was being held with No. 4 Group in Thailand. As before, the Red Cross were on hand to advise.

**WAR ORGANISATION
OF THE
BRITISH RED CROSS SOCIETY and ORDER OF ST JOHN
PRISONERS OF WAR DEPARTMENT**

11.1.1944

When replying please quote reference: FE/50186
Miss E.M. Lowe
Brook Cottage Farm,
Over Whitacre,
Coleshill,
Nr. Birmingham

Dear Miss Lowe
Thank you for your letter of 2.1.1944. We are very glad to fully realise what a great relief this must be to you. You should address letters as follows:

**PRISONERS OF WAR POST
SERVICE DES PRISONNIER DE GUERRE
49780741 SERGEANT E.B. ROBERTS
BRITISH PRISONER OF WAR CAMP
No. 4 P.O.W. CAMP
THAILAND**

May we suggest that you advise your fiancé's Records Office of his new camp address as we know that they are anxious to receive the latest information concerning the movements of prisoners of war.
Please do not hesitate to write to us at any time that you require information or advice.

Yours sincerely
S.G. King
Controller

P.S. The conditions prevailing in the Camps in Thailand are still not known as the Japanese refuse to allow the International Red Cross to visit there. The country is really very similar to that of Malaya. Mail is known to have been received in the camps. If you are able to see a copy of the PoW journal, in the

> *January issue on page 12 there is an article 'Supplies to Siam' which may be of comfort to you. Siam was the old name for Thailand. We know that mail has been forwarded from Malay camps up to Thailand and as it is no great distance away it is most likely that your fiancé has received your letters.*

Despite the Red Cross's assurance, Eric was not in regular receipt of Eunice's letters. Her diary ends abruptly in mid-May 1944. This may have been around the time she joined the Women's Land Army; however, it is more likely that a diary is missing. Eunice kept a diary every year until she died in 1980. Nevertheless, from here until 1945 her reactions and thoughts are unknown.

Chapter 16

August 1943–March 1944: Kinsayo and Kinsayo North, Thailand

From Tonchan Spring Camp we moved north to a site high above the river and located in fairly open jungle. This was a clean site above the river and we established ourselves there with our old British Army tents and made ourselves fairly comfortable. I had a tent on the edge of the camp site near to an animal track which went down to the river. I made myself as comfortable as possible with a bed made from bamboo. The CO had a small tent not far away and one night when it was dark, the CO had some sort of a lamp lit inside. As one of our men went by he saw the CO's shadow on the tent wall and he was standing on a small stool. The man, thinking this was a bit odd, went into the tent and found the CO standing on a stool faced by a cobra. The cobra was killed but this was the only incident I knew of involving snakes. Pythons were seen from time to time and I remember sharing in a stew made from one of these. It was alright and the meat tasted something like chicken (bland). By comparison with other places it was a good site and we set about digging latrines and getting everything in an orderly fashion. We were only on this site for a few weeks, whilst work was being done on the nearby rail track.

It was assumed that there was some sort of ration allowance for PoWs and the Japs would purchase rice, vegetables and other things from traders down river. Knowing the ethos of the area, I have no doubt that some of the money was diverted into Jap and other pockets. Added to that, for those in very remote locations, some of the supplies could have been lost en route. The evidence was that the farther we went from areas of civilisation, the poorer rations became. However, the Japs and the Koreans seemed to do reasonably well. On one occasion I was called upon to find a man to help in the Jap cookhouse, a job which no one willingly would do.

> There was a man from the 1/Cambridgeshires who volunteered to do the work. He was a tall, very hairy man who had attached himself to the little group I was part of. From what he said, the Japs fed well and occasionally he brought a little food for us from the Jap rations.

In a post-war letter to George White, Eric identifies this man as 'Buckingham' and that he managed to obtain some kidneys from the cookhouse. The Japanese and Koreans preferred meat to offal, so this was sometimes available. George White commented that 'The kidneys were nearly spoilt by me in cooking in a wok. Eric frequently laid this near disaster at my door.' There were two men with the surname Buckingham in the 1/Cambridgeshires who were captured at Singapore and interned in the same camp as Eric, so positive identification is not possible.

> After being there for a few weeks, we were told that we were to move again, still north. On the move our problem was always food and my friend, George White, and I managed to buy about twenty-seven small duck eggs for the journey. These came from a Thai trader on the river and we boiled these. That night we were told that we were only moving across the river. We sat looking at our eggs, eventually eating one and then another. In the process of an hour or two all the eggs had been eaten.

The 'eating of the eggs' was a memorable incident but neither George nor Eric could agree on when it happened. George White recalled that

> From Tonchan, we were taken up river in sampans to a small riverside camp for a short while, where little was done; from there we set out on foot to move to Kinsayo Main Camp. Eric and I were concerned that we had insufficient food available for this move and we somehow obtained about a dozen or more eggs which we hard-boiled and took with us. For some reason or other, the party stopped overnight in a jungle clearing and Eric and I decided that we ought to eat the eggs as we thought they would deteriorate in the heat, so we ate them all at one go! I don't think we suffered any ill effects. I agree that Eric and I ate all the eggs; this occurred on our move from the small riverside camp after Tonchan Spring Camp.

When we arrived at Kinsayo Main Camp, the four of us were broken up as far as occupying the same huts etc. and the same applied at the next camp, Kinsayo North Camp. This was largely due to canteen purchases needing to be in a reasonably secure location, necessitating Dixon and I sleeping where the eggs, tobacco, etc. was kept. Kinsayo North Camp was the furthest camp up the railway which we reached.

At Wampo we acquired some money from the members of the SSVF and the FMSVF as already told. 2500 dollars of this was given to me for safe keeping. Had the Japs found this upon me I would have been in serious trouble; they would have assumed the worst. I wore hose tops and I carried this money in the turned-down tops of these. One day I had the money in the pocket of an old shirt and wearing this I went into the jungle to collect wood. It was cold when I set out with the shirt on but as the temperature rose I took the shirt off and placed it on a tree stump. Our camp had a perimeter fence with a guard post at the only exit and that night I discovered I had left my shirt plus the money in the jungle. Under those circumstances anything is of value and likely to be picked up, even an old shirt. I avoided the guard and went back to where I had left the shirt and there it was. I was greatly relieved and got back into camp without being seen.

There was little or no meat and we were anxious to acquire some protein. It was arranged that a Jap guard with several PoWs would go down river to try and get a few water buffalo with this money. The outcome of this was to obtain thirty or forty water buffalo and drive them back up river. A corral was made in the jungle and we managed to keep our herd together due to one buffalo, he was an albino; we could manage him and the others followed. We killed a buffalo every few days; the meat was very tough but after stewing for about twenty-four hours, at least there was some good gravy. Then rather foolishly, the albino was killed and the rest of the herd broke out of their corral and were lost. The buffalo were slaughtered by tying the head to a tree and getting a Jap to fire into the front of the skull. The Japs very often did not make much of a job of this but we had a butcher who would then leap in with an axe and complete the job.

In his official report Lieutenant Colonel Lilly makes no mention of 'water buffalo', only cows. Local cows have horns and would have reminded Eric of buffaloes.

> On one occasion in the early evening, my friend George and I with a few others were in an old British Army tent when a Jap guard came in, beckoned to George and me to follow him. We were taken to the hut occupied by the guards and for no apparent reason forced to stand in a drainage ditch about two feet deep. I noticed the guard at first was wearing rubber boots and he returned, having changed them for leather boots. He brought with him a dozen others all wearing leather boots. We were then accused of not saluting a Jap Officer and we said we had not seen one, being in a tent. This carried no weight and they all set about kicking and beating us as we stood in the trench. The guards were obviously enjoying the process but fortunately our CO was told of what had happened and he arrived with a Japanese-speaking PoW. It seemed that a senior member of the Jap guard asserted his authority and we were allowed to go. This was typical of many incidents and the Japs enjoyed inflicting pain.

George White had no recollection of this incident. It was either another man or, as this was a particularly traumatic experience, Eric 'added' his friend in his memory and was alone at the time.

> I was awakened one night and had to hold myself on my bed to prevent being thrown off. It was an earthquake and the tremors were followed by violent winds. We heard at this camp that the Thai side of the railway had linked with the section being built from the Burma side at a pass in the mountain range which divided the two countries. This pass was known as 'Three Pagodas' from the three pagodas which were there. There being no railway work, life became a little easier and we were made to cut tree branches from the jungle and screen our camp from the sight of the railway. Apparently a Jap general was coming to officially open the line at Three Pagodas, where a ceremonial section of brass railway line had been laid. We were given a day's holiday and had to hide ourselves and the camp

from the railway when the Jap General went up to celebrate the linking of the Burmese and Thai sections of the railway. I saw the General go by in an inspection car. It was about this time, due to beriberi etc. that the Jap General is reputed to have said that '*Orru* [all] prisoner big bean.' We then had a period with almost nothing but peas and beans.

The two lines of the railway met on 17 October 1943. The section below describes part of the journey from Kinsayo to Kinsayo North Camp and was part of a short story, *Jungle Green*, typed by Eric in the 1950s or 1960s.

> Surely there must be some other way! Surely no-one, least of all these weak emaciated creatures, could be expected to haul their few possessions and their pain-wracked frames over this flimsy, swaying apology for a bridge. The narrow-gauge railway track took up the whole of the room and there were no hand-rails to which one could cling whilst inching one's way at this great height over the rushing torrent and jagged rocks below. Ah, apparently one could descend by a tortuous path, almost enveloped by the undergrowth and in the steaming heat to the river bed and find a spot to wade across, then climb painfully up the other side of the gorge – either way was hazardous in the extreme – so he chose the bridge; and now, as he studied where best to put his feet, he became aware of the Japanese soldier who straddled the path in front of him; there he stood, holding his rifle and bayonet across his body with both hands, his legs were stretched out and each boot was pressing against the inside of the railway line and with not the slightest intention of changing his stance. The soldier refused to let him continue. With all his belongings, the slightest movement from the soldier would have had him off the bridge and in the water below. To go forward meant squeezing by him on a few inches of slippery sleeper – but to go back? Oh no! He couldn't face THAT! Rather than turn back, he started to walk on the ends of the sleepers, but the sleepers were slippery and he only had a small amount of sleeper to step on. He decided to get on his hands and knees and went by the soldier in that way, clutching the sleeper ends. So, inch by inch and taking his life in his hands, he pressed on and, bathed in perspiration, he was relieved to get to the other side.

One or two other men followed me but the majority went through the water. The Jap on the bridge was challenging me and had I turned round and gone back he would have won but being forced to go by him on my hands and knees on the sleeper ends was a bit of a come-down for me.

We moved on foot to a camp farther north – Kinsayo North. This camp had been established some time before and the conditions we found there were appalling. There were the usual bamboo and *attap* huts and there were many sick men within them, sanitation was bad and it was obvious that many men failed to use the latrines provided, such as they were. There was excrement everywhere. The senior British Officer there was a lieutenant colonel from the 148th Field Regiment Royal Artillery, who still wore his dress cap which had a bright red band to it. The newcomers christened him 'cock robin'. [The 148th was the Bedfordshire Yeomanry Field Artillery Regiment. They arrived as reinforcements in early 1942. The lieutenant colonel was Stanley Wakefield Harris (44513), born in 1895 and enlisted in 1915. On his liberation questionnaire he listed his private address as 'Cavalry Club, London'. He returned home in 1945.] Our own CO, being senior, took authority. Lieutenant H.H. Bushell set about digging fresh latrines and we took over and cleaned up the camp, attending to the sick and inculcating some sensible discipline. [This was Lieutenant Hubert Henry Bushell (180398) of the 80th Anti-Tank Regiment of Artillery, who returned home in 1945.] Matters improved and the abominable smell which greeted us on our arrival was dispersed.

One of my jobs was to maintain records and claim on a ten-day basis for 10 cents per man for those who worked; the sick had nothing. However, I was told on my arrival that all men were paid 10 cents irrespective of whether they worked or were sick and that I should do the same. I duly did this and was sent for by the Japs who told me that by claiming pay for sick men I had set out to defraud the Japanese Imperial Army. There was some discussion and a lot of shouting and the outcome was that I had been summarily sentenced to be beheaded. I was told to stand aside and wait for the act to be committed. Fortunately at that point a Jap Lieutenant arrived on the scene. He was known to me and quite a good fellow. He enquired what was happening, turned to me and told me to leave. I left without delay and heard nothing more, but my figures had to be corrected. I went in search of the man (a Royal Artillery Sergeant) who had told me that in this camp all men were paid the 10 cents including the sick. Apparently on this occasion he had claimed only for the working men but he had not bothered to tell me. It seemed that the Jap Guard had been fiddling (probably in conjunction with the PoW), but when others arrived in the camp they decided to change their habit.

It is possible that Lieutenant Hattari was the 'Jap Lieutenant' who saved Eric from execution. However, it could have been the Japanese commander at this camp, Lieutenant Ouschiama. Lieutenant Colonel Lilly noted Ouschiama was; 'reasonable, polite and took an interest in the camp'. Pavillard (1962) describes Lieutenant Hattari as being 'a curious man. He spoke perfect English, he loved playing bridge, he was fond of quoting Gray's *Elegy* and, more unaccountably, a number of old political speeches by Lloyd George. He was a lawyer by profession and taught at the University of Tokyo.' I also recall Eric telling me that the Japanese Lieutenant was a Christian and believed this execution was unnecessary.

George White also had cause to remember Kinsayo North, which he recalled

> was in a shocking state. It was here that I was slightly knocked about for not saluting Lieutenant Hattari as he left the camp, but I don't remember Eric being involved. I know someone else was forced to stand with me in front of the guardroom, and that Lieutenant Ward on enquiring why we were there also got lined up. It was here also that the rats were permanent and there were dollars for medical purchases. [Second Lieutenant Kenneth W. Ward (187805) of the 1/5 was relatively young, born in 1922, and came from Nottingham. He survived and was repatriated in 1945.]

Near to our camp was a Jap food store for their troops. It had surrounding it a trench two metres deep, two metres wide at the top and one metre wide at the bottom. This had a triple purpose: (a) to keep out intruders; (b) as a drain; (c) to keep out rats. The Japs were very concerned about the rats getting at their food store and offered the PoWs 5 cents for every rat's tail produced. The rats, in their effort to get into the Jap food store, would fall into the trench when they were chased and killed. Lots were dug out and in about three days the Japs were presented with 2500 rats' tails. After that I think our chaps lost interest.

Although it was complete, I don't think the railway line was of any great use to the Japs. By now the war was going against them in Burma and US B-24 bombers followed our railway track through the jungle and bombed it at will, bridges in particular. From this camp we went down country on the railway but on top of steel railway vans which were already loaded with Jap stores of various sorts, oil, etc. The railway vans had semi-circular roofs and it was not an easy thing, with all our belongings, to stay up there. I remember that all I had to stop me from falling off was my heel jammed against a steel rivet head. However, part of this journey was by river and we saw one or two of the camps we had previously occupied. The jungle had already crept back in and it was obvious that before long (with the help of termites and other things) evidence of our being there would be lost. At one stage of our journey we crossed over the semi-circular trestle bridge at south Wampo. This was a hair-raising experience and we shook hands with each other before the train was on the bridge. There was a loco at the back and one at the front. Halfway across the bridge, the signalling system between the two loco drivers seemed to go awry. The lead one was supposed to be pulling and the rear one pushing but the two started to fight for the train. Much to our relief we managed to get to the other side.

Mail was a rarity but on two or three occasions we were allowed to send a printed postcard home. This gave our name and indicated certain things such as 'I am well/ill', 'I am working for pay' and other nonsensical items. On two or three occasions I received mail from home. This had been accumulated by the Japs and once I received a batch of thirty letters, all very old by that time.

Chapter 17

Home Front: March 1944–June 1945

In July 1944 Aunt Lilian received another postcard from Eric. The format was different and was of the type described by Eric at the end of the last chapter. The new format had pre-printed phrases that could be crossed out and a few words added. The Japanese wanted to prevent PoWs from sending any coded messages home. It also reduced the need for Japanese translators and censors. It did little more than confirm that Eric was still alive and in the absence of anything else, even this was a cause for celebration.

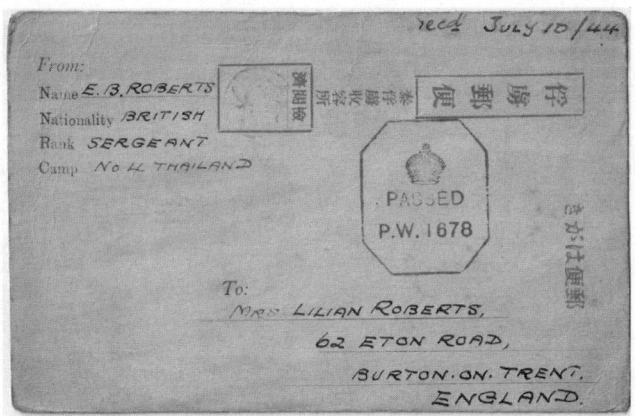

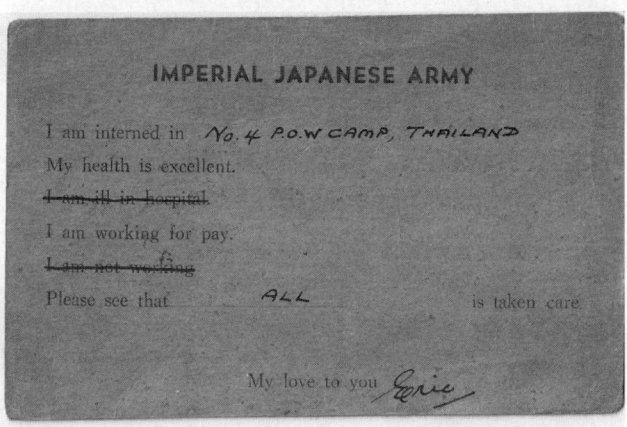

In 1944 it was determined that a number of PoWs would be transported to the Japanese mainland for forced labour. The men of the 1/5 chosen were among the fittest and were transported to Singapore to board two ships: the *Rakuyo Maru* and the *Kachidoki Maru*. As the ships were carrying PoWs they could have been legitimately marked with the Red Cross. They were not. As such, on 12 September 1944 they came under attack by the USN and were sunk by two US submarines (the USS *Sealion* and USS *Pampanito*). Out of the 2,217 PoWs on board the vessels, an estimated 1,159 lost their lives. However, a number of PoWs survived and were rescued by the USN. The rescued British prisoners were repatriated to the UK via the USA and arrived home in late 1944. There was considerable interest in any information that they could impart as so little had been released about the camps during the war.

One of the survivors was Private Joseph Bagnall (4974519). He lived in Burton-on-Trent and his return was reported in the *Burton Mail* in late 1944. Naturally, Aunt Lilian did not know whether Eric was involved in this incident. If he was, had he perished or survived? Aunt Lilian wrote to Mrs Bagnall in the hope that her husband could tell her about Eric.

> *Oct 25 1944*
> *41 Coton Park*
> *Linton*
> *Burton-on-Trent*
>
> *Dear Mrs Degg,*
> *I received your letter this morning, which I am only pleased to tell you if I can, what you want to know. I know just how you feel, for I have felt that way myself, and I do hope you get better.*
> *I have had quite a few people inquiring about my husband's unit and things, anyway when he arrives home I'll ask him if he knows your boy. My husband was in the 1/5 Sherwoods, D Company. Also as a prisoner, was in No. 4 Camp, Thailand. Hoping you have the same news as me.*
> *I remain yours,*
> *Mrs. Bagnall*

Despite Private Bagnall's ordeal, the day after he returned home, he went to see Aunt Lilian to tell her about his time as a PoW, about Eric and to confirm that Eric was not on board either ship. Aunt Lilian wrote to Eunice to tell her about the meeting.

> 62 Eton Rd.
> Burton on Trent
> Tuesday
>
> Dear Eunice,
> I felt I must drop you a line (without waiting for one from you) as I have just had over an hour's visit from Private J. Bagnall, his wife and wife's father.
> Private Bagnall arrived home yesterday and was good enough to come and see me right away. But at any rate he was able to bring me good news that Eric was definitely <u>not</u> on that ship; and when last seen (which was about the first week in September) was alright, also Jim Parker, Wilf Wood and various others. They were left behind at Thailand and Private Bagnall does not think it likely they will be moved now, owing to Jap shipping problems. He says there is a good chance of them being rescued if our side can make a smash at Malaya and Singapore. So it is to be hoped that this will not be long delayed. Of course I asked all the questions I could think of (being utterly set back by the unexpected visit). I wish <u>you</u> could have been here to think of things I could not.
> Anyhow Private Bagnall has six weeks' leave, so we might be again in touch with him. Apparently Eric does clerical work connected with usual office routine and is in fairly good health considering all. I found that he had had malaria twice, but he said fairly mild attacks.
> Private Bagnall received <u>no</u> letters during the time he was a prisoner, but could not say about Eric as some had received about three he thought. I can tell you more when I see you, cannot stop for more now. It is a great relief, even this small bit of news.
>
> Lots of love,
> Aunty Lily

In late 1942, Jim Parker had been sent down the river due to serious illness. From his new location, somehow he was able to write a letter home containing news of Eric.

62 Eton Rd.
Burton on Trent
Wednesday

Dear Eunice,
You will be surprised to hear from me again so soon, but I must pass on to you the latest news – unless of course you have already heard it. It is no less than a <u>message</u> from Eric. It has come to one in a roundabout way; having indeed been brought to me last night by a neighbour (Mr Horobin) who is also our butcher.

It seems that recently Jim Parker's father received a <u>letter</u> from him (Jim) in which he asked that Mrs Degg should be told that Eric is quite alright, that they are <u>both together</u> and in <u>good</u> health. This message came to Mrs Matkin with whom JP lived in Derby St. and Mrs M. took it to Mr Horobin to pass on to me. Does all this sound <u>too</u> complicated for you? Of course <u>I</u> was all agog to know <u>why</u> JP should be able to write a letter at all to his father when apparently Eric cannot do so to us. Mrs Horobin has promised to see if she can get any other items of information from Mrs Matkin and she will then let me know.

She wonders if by any chance the Salvation Army might be in touch with the camps and thus have been able to get a letter through for JP but this is of course pure surmise. I have been thinking that perchance by now for you may have heard that from Bette regarding this as of course she would be sure to have heard but knowing her propensity for procrastination I wouldn't bank on that. I felt terribly bucked and this seems to mean more than that postcard. Don't <u>you</u> think so?

Oh! Well, I will stop for more now, as I want Aunty Rose to drop this in the post for me.

Lots of love
<u>Aunty Lily</u>

Bette was again in touch at the end of the year to say that she had received a printed postcard from Jim.

> *21 Glasgow Road*
> *Paisley*
> *<u>Scotland</u>*
> *<u>22nd Dec. 1944</u>*
>
> *My dear Eunice*
> *Just a few lines to tell you that I have received a card from Jim, and to thank you for your Xmas card. The card from Jim reads: 'Your Mails received with thanks. My health is good. I am working for pay. My best regards to Mother, Father, Reg. & Phyllis.' It is partly printed, but different to the previous cards which I have received. Have you also received one from Eric?*
>
> *Well Eunice I have copied the Life of a PoW and am returning it to you with thanks. Were you able to obtain Pte Bagnall's address for me? Mrs. Cook has written to me twice, and I haven't replied to her letter as I have been waiting to hear from you.*
>
> *I read in the paper last night that a number of British PoWs in Siam had been killed by RAF raids, but it said Central Siam, so I trust the 'nibs' were miles away from there. I also wrote to the Red Cross today asking for particulars about the ten-word cable which we can send once per year, so I shall get it off as soon as I hear further.*
>
> *Now Eunice I have stacks of work to do, so forgive this letter being so short. Cheerio for now.*
>
> *Yours affectionately,*
> *<u>Bette</u>*

The reference to 'the Life of a PoW' relates to the account of PoW life produced by Mrs Hope Robinson (see Appendix). Bette also mentions a 'ten-word cable' which could be sent once per year. No such cables were ever received by the PoWs.

In late December 1944 Aunt Lilian received another postcard from Eric. It had taken six months to arrive. Short of confirming that he was alive, it provided little information.

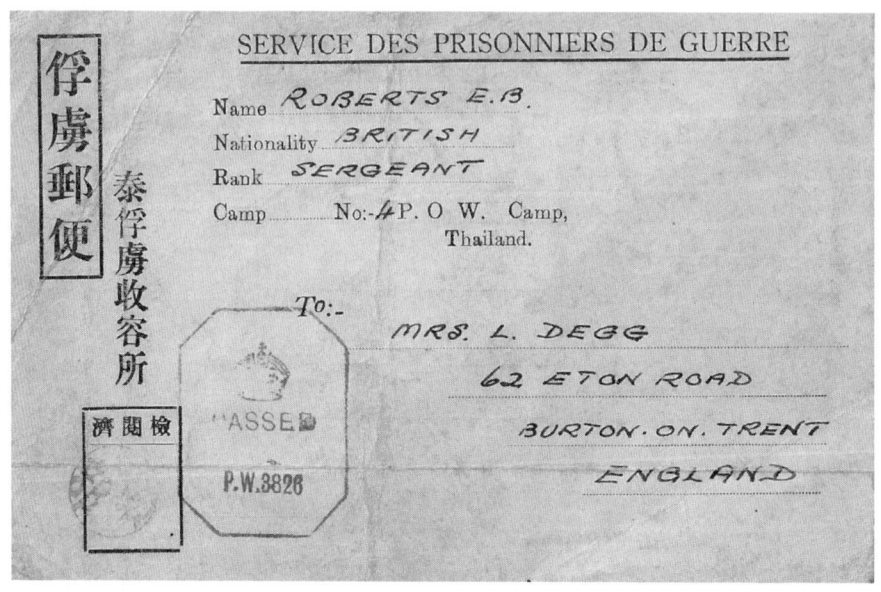

Chapter 18

March 1944–June 1945: Tamuan, Thailand

We were now into 1944, the railway being finished, back down the line we were sent, we left the train at Kanchanaburi and marched along the road towards Banpong [*sic*]. However, a few miles along we went onto a camp site where a few huts had already been erected. There was no cover for us and I bedded down that night and for several nights under a tree. It was now obvious that a lot of PoWs were being brought off the railway and there was an uneasiness amongst the Japs. The camp we had arrived at was called Tamuan.

George White recalled that:

It became a very big camp eventually, but for a long time the four of us occupied the same hut. Here Eric was mostly engaged in the camp office and I with an Australian, Mick Rowe, occupied a separate canteen building, which opened as a shop in the evenings. [There was no one with the name 'Michael Rowe' in the Australian forces at this time. Positive identification of this man is not possible. 'Mick' may have been a nickname and/or the surname different. Alternatively, he may have been an Australian serving with the volunteer forces.]

On this site might have been a small village, there were still one or two occupied huts and a well. We arrived in the evening and there were some very pleasant scents arising from the miscellaneous collection of trees around. It was said that it had been a monastic garden. The river was some distance away, being wide and shallow. I now went down with malaria and my good friend George watched over me for about four days. In previous camps our CO had always been the senior officer and I had kept an eye on the administrative side of things. My friend George came to me as I lay under a tree with malaria and said 'The b...s are taking over.' By now numerous men had arrived including a large party from Tarsao for whom I had no regard. I got up and went to the hut which was being used as a camp office, asserted my authority and took over. As the weeks went on we eventually had in the camp about 5000 British (which included 150 Americans who were attached to us), 2000 Aussies and 2000 Dutch. Working parties went out each day and a Jap store was established a little way down the road.

By now there was more air activity and the Japs insisted that we remain under cover when planes were around. The Jap store a little way off was bombed and that night we had a roll call by the light of the fires from that. Things were becoming a bit tricky.

George White went into more detail:

At Tamuan, we saw from a distance one day considerable air activity. We could tell they weren't Jap planes as there was some ack-ack fire. That was the day the RAF bombed the Kwai Bridge. Also at Tamuan, on one occasion, allied bombers returning from a mission further south flew over the camp with open bomb doors low enough for us to see the crew waving to us. The Koreans went mad trying to get us back into our huts.

Whilst at Tamuan a small amount of Red Cross goods were received. This was local purchase stuff. We were amused to find that two pairs of boxing gloves had been sent. Our friendly Jap Interpreter announced that he considered boxing was a cruel blood sport and the prisoners were not to have the gloves. The two pairs of boxing gloves lay in the Jap guard hut until one night a couple of Japs put them on and started sparring with each other. Tempers became frayed, an iron bar was produced and one Jap lay dead. The dead Jap was known by us as 'Madam Butterfly' – he was very pale and an absolute shocker. Whenever he was present there was trouble and someone was badly beaten. We were overjoyed to hear the news and from then on things were a little better in the camp. It appeared that 'Madam Butterfly' had worked in Malaya before the war and members of the SSVF and FMSVF were sent to round up enemy aliens. He was one of them and when arrested they put him in a steel railway van, intending to collect him later (the van door was latched from the outside). A day or two later he was found and when the tables were turned and the Japs overran Singapore, he was released and set out on a vendetta which continued until his death.

A number of unfortunate incidents occurred at Tamuan. It was obvious that information was being given to the Japs. We had a Bombardier Squires with us who was a wizard with radio and if we could get dry batteries from the traders on the river, he would quietly put his radio bits together and with luck tune in to New Delhi. [This was Bombardier Denis Gaston Squires (916702) of the 148th Field Regiment of Artillery from Walton-on-the-Naze; he survived and returned home in 1945.] Had the Japs discovered this there would have been serious trouble. I was only marginally concerned with this; the less anyone knew about it the better. After the war, my friend George reminded me that on one occasion I came to him and told him that the radio was buried in the ground beneath where we both slept. There were perhaps 9000 men in that camp and that day Japs came and dug in the ground over which we slept. George was there at the time; I was elsewhere. George told me he was in a state of panic but the Japs found nothing. George told me that later when he challenged me I said 'Oh! It had been moved, didn't I tell you?'

George White also noted this incident:

Eric passed on bits of news from the secret radio from time to time. On one occasion he told me, at lights out, that the radio was hidden under our sleeping bay. Unwelcome news as far as I was concerned. Early next morning the Japs started a search and for a long time I sat in the parade ground waiting for the radio's discovery. All went well; however, as soon as the search ended I found Eric and learned that it had been removed to a safe hiding place during the night!

There was one man, a Eurasian, although he claimed not, was known to be giving information to the Japs on PoW affairs (he spoke Jap). Almost always if he appeared on the scene to act as interpreter, trouble ensued. Death was not uncommon and four of us met to discuss what should be done with this man. It was agreed that we would dispose of him, probably with poison and we parted with the intention of arranging details later. Fortunately, we were able to arrange to send him down river and I never saw him again.

At Tamuan, the CO (Lieutenant Colonel Lilly) was beaten up by the Japs. He came to me after his experience and accused me of being responsible because I had given information away to the Japs. I denied this for I knew nothing about it but Lieutenant Colonel Lilly said it was so because Captain MacDonald had said so. The latter was a man I knew and was acting as British Group Adjutant in the camp. I went to MacDonald and repeated what the CO had said to me. MacDonald said he knew that I was not guilty but he, MacDonald, was not going to carry the can. Such things occurred to me on several occasions. [This was Captain James MacDonald (229043) of the 3rd Anti-Aircraft Regiment of Artillery from Petersfield, Hants. He survived and returned home in 1945.]

In January 1945, our CO came to me one evening and said that all commissioned officers were to be taken away from the camp by 0900 hrs the following morning. It had been arranged with the Japs that warrant officers and non-commissioned officers would take over the responsibilities which had been those of the Officers. As stated before, the British Group was then 5000 strong and he gave me the name of the Warrant Officer First Class (WO1) who would be the OC. He added that I should be the British Group Adjutant. His final comment was 'If you don't run things the Japs will.' [The WO1 was Regimental Sergeant Major Victor Charles Christopher (1055584) of the 9th Coast Regiment Royal Artillery from London.]

There were rather a lot of commissioned officers and based on the assumption that they were not to be engaged on manual tasks, I suppose an additional burden had been placed upon the rest of us who were not defined in that way. WOs and NCOs in the British Army play a very important role and it was something of a joke that commissioned officers who maintained their superiority would turn on their heels and depart, saying something like 'Carry on, Sarn't', or 'Sarn't Major', as the case might be. Generally, it was the WOs and NCOs who maintained discipline; there were some duds but there were also some very good ones whose reputation was known. So I was not unduly concerned about the departure of the majority of the commissioned officers but I was particularly concerned about the loss of a few, Lieutenant Colonel Lilly in particular, who had been a very brave man and so far as I knew had never shirked his responsibilities.

The number of Jap guards was never very great; in fact it would have been very easy for the PoWs to take over the camp. However, with the nearest allied troops over 1000 miles through very difficult terrain, we needed the Japs in order to survive. Conversely, the Japs needed us to organise our own affairs within the camps. So a senior British Officer would emerge as a subsidiary camp commandant and he would have an adjutant. Records had to be maintained and clerical work done for Jap purposes which called for some clerical staff. Sanitation was a matter of great importance when thousands of men were confined to a clearing in the jungle. Men were needed for this.

There was a lot of work involved in feeding 5000 men, even on meagre rations. Everything had to be cooked, rice, vegetables and meat if the latter was available. Quite a few cooks were needed. Cooking facilities were very primitive. Things like very large woks were used; these were built up off the ground and fired from beneath. Fuel had to be found on a daily basis and large quantities of water were required. It is likely that 6pts per man per day, which for 5000 men amounted to 3750 gallons per day and whilst at Tamuan the river was quite a distance away. Water had to be carried in 4-gallon cans (probably used originally for kerosene) and these were in general use in that area. Three or four cans would be carried on a pole between two men, although at one stage we had a hand truck which was pulled and pushed by four men. NCOs were required to be in charge of all these activities. Food had to be distributed and this needed supervising to ensure fairness. The huts and the camp generally had to be kept clean. Discipline had to be maintained and most WOs and NCOs still exercised their authority in accordance with rank. Every day the Japs called for working parties which accounted for all fit men apart from those on the various camp jobs.

A WO or NCO was leader of each working party. This was necessary to keep trouble with the Japs to a minimum. A WO or NCO was also placed in charge of each hut in which 150 men were quartered and normally calm reigned unless the Japs decided to cause trouble on some trumped-up matter. So, the departure of commissioned officers did not make much difference, the organisation was already there as it had been in normal army conditions. It was not a matter of giving and taking orders, it was a question of collaborating for the common good.

At Tamuan, I put the report on Japanese atrocities in a sealed metal box and buried it at a known place in the camp office hut which was near the boundary fence, not far from the Kanburi/Banpong [*sic*] road. One of our men for no apparent reason was found by the fence and shot dead by a guard.

According to records from the war crimes trials held after the war, this was Fusilier Leonard William Wanty (4272350) of the 9th Battalion, Royal Northumberland Fusiliers. He was 25 years old. On the night of New Year's Eve 1944, Fusilier Wanty had been visiting a friend's hut. A curfew at 2300 hrs was in operation, and a bugle call was sounded. Wanty heard this and left his friend's hut to return to his own. He met one of the Korean sentries who proceeded to escort him to Wanty's hut. On the way they met Major Totaro Mizutani and Ensign Tsumura. The Korean guard was asked why Fusilier Wanty had not been shot on sight for being out after curfew, at which point Major Mizutani took the guard's rifle and shot Fusilier Wanty at a range of 3 metres. After the war, the murder of Fusilier Wanty was one of three charges brought against Major Totaro Mizutani. He was found guilty of all three charges and was executed at Changi Jail (Mizutani Trial, Case No. 65080).

> Some chaps did silly things and probably became involved with local people, either selling or buying. The Japs became rather edgy and the following day all the huts including the camp office were demolished and moved back from the boundary. The men were also moved back farther into the camp. The ground where the huts had stood was then, under the orders of the Japs, dug up for the purpose of making a garden and growing some vegetables. I became a little worried at the prospect of the Japs finding the report on their atrocities. I spoke to the men on the digging and asked them to keep a sharp eye open for my metal box. Fortunately, it was not found.

There was now increased Allied air activity and we were told by the Japs that we were to move. We duly went back to the railway, on top of railway wagons already loaded with materials coming from the north. That night was spent at Nakom Paton, at a camp which had been established as a base hospital for those working on the railway. The buildings there were constructed from timber but damage had been caused by bombing. We spent the night in the open and had some rice.

By now there was evidence of Jap wounded from Burma. Some of these were seen on the railway sitting in railway vans with nothing; they seemed to be in a wretched condition and our guards treated them harshly. Wounded Japs were also in the camp at Nakom Paton and there were those who begged food from us. They received more sympathy from the PoWs than the Japs. One or two who were caught giving food were beaten, also the wounded Japs. This was another illustration of the Jap character.

The following day, back on the railway and on top of loaded vans, we proceeded to where a steel bridge across a ravine with a river running had been bombed. The locals had constructed a footbridge of sorts from liana and bamboo, the lianas supporting a board; well, not so much a plank as a cane, really, and slippery at that. [Lianas are long, flexible, parasitic plants which are rooted in the ground and grow on the sides of trees.] It was about 12 inches wide and provided a walkway – the whole structure sagged badly. The supporting lianas had been fixed to the shattered ends of the bridge on either bank. The whole thing was swaying and seemed to be moving up and down. I stood and saw the party clamber up the railway embankment and one by one the weary ones inched their way across, with some uncertainty, carrying their bits and pieces which meant life to them. All having crossed, I set off myself with all my possessions and noticed with dismay that two 4-gallon cooking pots had been abandoned by those who had been detailed to carry them; this was both unpardonable and unthinkable. Knowing that without the pots, cooking would be difficult, there was nothing else for it and I picked up the pots, one in each hand, and made my trembling way across the dreaded bridge – with a cooking pot in each hand. To start with I was running downhill and then there was a steep climb to the other side. I tried not to look down into the torrent beneath and, having completed the job, felt rather proud of myself. I later had a few words with those who had abandoned the pots.

We were directed to some land to the side of the track where we were to spend the night. I climbed down the railway embankment and was faced with an area with quite a number of trees.

The following incidents from the short story *Jungle Green* occurred at this point:

> He was heartily sick of the sights and sounds of the jungle: day after weary day they had plodded on, the tattered remains of clothing clinging to their emaciated bodies, their feet sore and blistered and ill-shod: all their worldly goods were carried on their backs, threadbare shirts, scraps of blanket and the cooking pot that was the clue to survival here in this dark, steaming hell. Suddenly he was aware of the silence: normally there was an incessant chatter and a constant stirring in the undergrowth through which they had to hack their way, but here it was comparatively easy going with humps and hollows underfoot, albeit that ominous silence all around. He felt a vague unease before he even noticed that the only vegetation in the area seemed to be a superfluity of mangroves. Surely he had never known what weariness was before and most of his companions had the appearance of skeletal sleepwalkers. Many of them, he knew, would never recover from this nightmare.
>
> Ah, blessed relief – nightfall and a brief respite from grim reality; he looked carefully about him and was smitten again with the same sense of foreboding at the eeriness of the spot; the ground was ridged like the sands of the sea shore when the tide has receded, and whereas most of his fellow prisoners were choosing the comparative comfort of the hollows in which to lay their worn out frames, he found a fairly high hillock and was soon fast asleep. For these men, being driven remorselessly on by their Japanese captors, sleep was their only escape into blessed oblivion and maybe, if they were lucky, pleasant dreams of happier times. All too soon the night was over and he awoke; at about 2.30 am the tide came in and now there was silence no longer, but the rushing and gurgling of water as the tidal river advanced and the oaths and exclamations of those who had been trapped in their comfortable little hollows; little bundles of this and that and the odd cooking pot were floating around amidst the flounderings and clutchings of their owners, whilst he on his hillock allowed himself the almost unknown privilege of a chuckle – which ended almost hysterically as his eyes swept the scene.

Quite early the following morning I saw a number of the locals crossing the bridge and amongst them were two Chinese men carrying a huge tractor tyre threaded onto a bamboo cane which they carried on their shoulders with apparent composure. At the sight of these, my pride of the previous day became deflated. I was not the eighth wonder after all.

I suppose we had something to eat, probably rice with tea. Then our job was to unload the train we had arrived on which was on the far side of the destroyed bridge, move the goods down the river bank to boats which were moved across the river to the far bank. Unload the boats, carry the goods up the far bank and load again onto railway wagons. Most of the trainload was oil in 40-gallon drums, not very easy for men to handle. When the Japs discovered that quite a few of the drums had been holed and were leaking, we were forced to carry the drums on stretchers made from rice bags and bamboo poles. Eventually the work was done and we were back on top of the railway vans or trucks, on to a railway marshalling yard on the edge of Bangkok where we arrived in the evening.

The yard had been bombed and much damage had been done. When night came the Japs departed and left us to our own devices, knowing I suppose that an air raid was likely. American bombers duly arrived and I crawled under a railway wagon and lay down between the railway lines. I suppose everyone did the same. I remained there until first light when I emerged to view the scene. Lengths of railway line had been lifted by the bombing and were sticking endways up in the ground. Fortunately, we had no casualties. When it was safe to do so, the Japs returned. We were then taken to the river nearby where we were pushed onto two river boats. The boat I was on became very crowded and in the end I had only one foot on the deck; it was not possible to get the other one down on the deck. I was pleased that the journey by river was fairly short and at dusk we arrived at a concrete dock, along which ran a number of warehouses (or *godowns* as they are known in those parts). We climbed up concrete steps onto the dock and were directed into one of the warehouses. By now it was dark and I felt around and found some sandbags. I settled down for the night against these. The following morning I awoke to find myself looking through a large hole in the roof and silhouetted against the early morning sky were the fins of a very large bomb. This was identified as a US blockbuster (unexploded). I suppose this was a Jap idea of a joke, for overnight the Japs had disappeared again. We spent several nights around the bomb but none of the PoWs appeared unduly perturbed. [The 'blockbuster' would have ranged in size from approximately 4,000lb (1,800kg) to 12,000lb (5,400kg).]

Chapter 19

June–August 1945: Pratchai, Thailand

After a few days' work on various things, we moved once again to a small town called Pratchai. 3000 of the British Group were detached and sent elsewhere (I believe on some airfield construction), leaving me as one of the remaining 2000. We went to a camp at Pratchai with 1000 Dutch and 1000 Australians. Also, a large part of the camp was occupied by a Jap regiment of artillery. Overlooking the camp were hills upon which stood a Buddhist temple decorated in brilliant blue and gold (that is what it seemed like from below). I understood that this was a place of pilgrimage for the King of Thailand and whilst the majority of the road from Bangkok to it was very rough, within a short distance of the temple the road developed into a well-made one. We were engaged on a variety of work including the making of gun emplacements in the hills above the camp, the guns being trained upon our camp.

The significance of the comment 'the guns being trained upon our camp' should not be underestimated. Russell (1958) stated that: During the last six months of the conflict unmistakably clear orders were issued from the War Ministry itself by the Vice-Minister of War, Shibayama, to prevent our prisoners from falling into Allied hands. The order stated, among other things, that the policy for the 'handling of prisoners of war in these times, when the situation is becoming more pressing, and the evils of war extend to the Imperial Domain and other places, will be found in the enclosed summary. We hope that you will follow it, making no mistakes.' The 'policy' was described in the enclosure as being to make every effort, and spare no pains 'to prevent the prisoners of war from falling into the enemy's hands.'

There was a feeling that things were not going too well for the Japs and on the 15 August 1945 the Jap Camp Commandant said that the war was over due to something he could not describe. We heard later that he was referring to the atom bomb. However, I heard later from General Slim that the Japs had been beaten in Burma – and were on the run before that event. So, the ex-PoWs took over the camp they were in, the Jap Artillery Regiment departed, and the Korean element of the guard also went from the camp.

George White recalled of 15 August 1945:

The last camp, Pratchai, was the scene of the great day. Rumours had been circulating of the steady advances of the 14th Army to Rangoon, and we wondered what action the Japs would take if Malaya was invaded. On the day, a party of PoWs was marched out of camp in the process of being transferred to another camp, thus reducing our numbers. They left early in the morning. Later we observed the Nips (billeted in huts across the parade ground in the same camp as us) taking wicker baskets to a dump and burning their contents. Then in the afternoon, the party, which had left in the morning, returned with tales of chaos reigning in the other camp. At about the same time Regimental Sergeant Major Christopher was called to the Jap commandant's hut. A few minutes later he reappeared with thumbs high in the air and we knew it was all over. Within minutes, flags appeared: the Union Flag, the Stars and Stripes and a Dutch flag. We were free. [The Union Flag was used again in 2001; see Epilogue.]

Next to our camp was a Jap store containing food and a variety of other things; we had access to this which was fortunate. We were anxious that there should be no clash between the Japs and the ex-PoWs and it was arranged that the Japs would maintain an armed guard on the store and the perimeter of our camp, not to keep ex-PoWs in but to keep others out. Having access to the food store, we had reasonable food. There was also clothing in the store, shirts and shorts, sufficient being found to equip our men. Without much delay we had contact with British forces in Burma in the shape of a paratrooper, Major Redman, who came into the camp in a Jeep. [Attempts to identify Major Redman have been unsuccessful. He may have been in the Scots Guards, but this is unconfirmed.] He said he had been with a party of British for some time in the jungle near to Kanchanaburi and was probably only a few miles from where we were in Tamuan.

George White elaborates on the reason for the presence of Major Redman:

An English Guards officer strolled into camp, having been in the area with a party of Thai supporters in case they were needed to prevent the Japs from trying to wipe us out if and when the Malayan invasion started. A large car battery came to hand and from the radio we learned of the atom bombs on Nagasaki and Hiroshima.

We had some discussions with Major Redman and he said he would arrange for an air drop of K-rations by Dakota. [By the end of the war air-dropping supplies to jungle forces was tried and tested, the RAF having supplied thousands of Allied troops operating behind Japanese lines. K-rations were a US invention, designed for mobile troops to be easy to carry and to provide three basic meals for a single day.] Also, if we could arrange a landing strip, the Dakota would take back thirty of our most sick men. Major Redman also suggested that an insecticide (DDT) would be a help to us and he would arrange for a 40-gallon drum on the same drop. We found a fairly flat stretch of land nearby and I went out with a party of men to fill in a few holes and cut down any obstructions. Major Redman said he thought it would be alright and the drop was arranged. I was on the site when the Dakota arrived. It made two or three passes and threw out the goods they had brought. There were no parachutes attached and it all fell to the ground with a thump, some packages bursting open. The 40-gallon drum of DDT was intact but when opened proved to be diesel. We had to drive off the local people who were trying to collect what they could for their own purposes. I was glad we had arranged for the Japs to maintain a guard on our camp. Having cleared the ground, the plane landed and we got our thirty sick men aboard. The plane then ran to the farthest point of our strip, turned and raced as hard as it could to the opposite end. I waited for it to crash into the trees but it managed to become airborne just in time.

However, it was decided that it was too risky to arrange for another landing. The goods which had arrived were loaded onto a Jap lorry and taken back to camp. We were all delighted with our K-rations and enjoyed a very welcome change in diet.

Following 15 August 1945, a lot happened. We had some very good WOs and senior NCOs who established their authority. Obviously, all the men were brought together and were told what would be occurring, movement to Bangkok, then Rangoon and eventually repatriation to the UK which may take some time. It was pointed out that they were now totally under British Army authority and indiscipline would not be tolerated. Necessary work in the camp must continue but they were permitted to leave the camp to visit the nearby small town of Pratchai or the pagoda, if they so wished. There was nothing of any great interest in the area and most men were content to take things easily and benefit from improved rations. Further sick men left by road for Bangkok and were probably then evacuated by air. The camp generally was very orderly. However, one little party of Australians managed to acquire a barrel of rice spirit which they brought back into camp. This was very powerful stuff and to avoid the consequence of drunkenness had to be taken from them. Earlier on we had tried to dig a well but having dug about 30' or 40' down without success, it was abandoned. The barrel of spirit was thrown down the well followed by a flaming length of bamboo from the cookhouse. There was a terrific roar of flame and the well collapsed. That was the end of the spirit and we had no more trouble. Apart from a few of our sick, the first men to leave the camp were the 150 Americans. These were followed by about 1000 Australians and our men followed in batches by road to Bangkok where they were quartered temporarily at the University.

On 30 August 1945, Eric sent his first real letters home. They were responses to letters written nine months earlier which he had received in November 1944.

Siam,
5 September 1945

Mrs. L. Degg,
62, Eton Road,
BURTON ON TRENT,
ENGLAND

My Dear Aunt

 I believe that now you will probably know more of me than I of you, for the last mail received, about the 18th of last month, was dated November 1944. Subsequent to that I am completely in the dark, but I do hope you and everyone are <u>well</u>. So far as I am concerned, am very fit and I think none the worse for the last three and a half years. Whilst things have not exactly been a picnic, I have been very lucky and the time, which of course has been a bitter waste, is not an absolute loss, for at least one has been given an insight into human nature and the capacity to appreciate simple pleasures. Also one has been taught to recognise disinterested services which have previously passed by unnoticed.

 I have spent my time with a very cosmopolitan lot having a variety of colours and tongues, but so far as the British and Australians are concerned they have stood up to the life very well. Their never-failing spirit and sense of humour under most difficult conditions has been admirable and is something which has served them in good stead.

 Most of my time has been spent in jobs of an administrative nature which have proved to be more agreeable than an excess of pick and shovel work, although I have had a shot or two at the latter.

 Food has presented its difficulties and although we have become accustomed to a 'native' diet will all be very glad for a change.

 For our captors – you will know all about them and I have reason to believe that many of them will be treated justly.

 It is unnecessary to say that you and all have been constantly in my thoughts. Many of your little bits of 'advice' have proved to be of sterling value.

 A very good friend of mine, George White, and I have religiously carried out your spot of witchcraft on the first of the month, the cutting of a piece of hair, although I must confess that on the first of <u>this</u> month it was completely overlooked. Incidentally, its benefits have been problematic and I haven't yet asked the Padre for his opinion.

 I was glad Bagnall came to see you, rather a rough diamond, but a very genuine man – an ex-miner as you will have gathered.

Further to mail, I have possibly had in all about a hundred postcards and letters, all of which have been six to twelve months old when received. This is due to being situated in out of the way spots (I spent about eighteen months in the jungle) and Japanese communications are notoriously bad plus an entire lack of interest on their part in respect of such matters as prisoners' welfare.

Enough of sordid details of the past, the future is all that matters. A large number of our fellows have already been flown out to India and I do not think it will be many weeks before we have all been moved.

This camp (I have been here since the end of June) is approximately 65 miles from Bangkok and communications with the capital by road and rail are quite fair, despite the fact that the latter is somewhat erratic and the former does not develop into a tarmacked surface until about eight kilometres from Bangkok.

Supplies of medicines, foodstuffs and newspapers have been dropped for us by air, and to us the perusal of the news sheets reveals a considerably changed world and we are forced to admit of a fellowship with Rip Van Winkle. The change of Govt. is a source of no little concern to us but the lack of preparatory information prevents obtaining a clear picture of conditions. At present 'it likes me not'.

I sincerely hope England is not becoming too Americanized, although the Americans I have met, with few exceptions, have been very decent fellows. The Americans seem to have been largely propagandized (a good word) by us, but maybe it is to some purpose. The recent arrangements concerning Lease and Lend appear to indicate this.

Delighted to hear of Ronald's daughter, seemingly you considered the name of the child was an unimportant detail, but after all I am practically her Uncle and one should know these things.

I cannot write more than one letter at present so this will have to serve for all. If I had have been able to have written more I think they would have all been duplicates one of the other for letter-writing to me seems almost a newly acquired art. Anyhow I hope shortly to regain proficiency and make up for lost time (not lost opportunity).

It is doubtful whether or not I shall be home for Michaelmas Day, something I very much regret but by that time I should be in some civilized place and it will be a date which will not be forgotten. I have celebrated this to date with several of my friends plus what meagre funds we possessed. 'My Aunt's Birthday' is quite a well-known event.

Please give Eunice my especial love and thank her for all her letters and the photographs. I regret her letters and postcards are not tied up with blue ribbon or anything of that nature; necessity has deemed that they be used for a variety of purposes but assure her that the photos are still intact (including one of you). Practically all my personal possessions were lost on Singapore Island together with what photos I had, and I was delighted to receive others.

My love to Mother and Dad and many thanks for their letters. I do hope Dad is better and carrying on. War time is a sufficient bogy without an additional one of sickness.

Also please give my love to Ronald, Barbara and Families and of course my congratulations to Ronald and Kate.

Don't worry!

Love
Eric

Through Major Redman, we had contact with British forces and a sort of liaison office was established in Bangkok. Quite early on a Jeep arrived in the camp with a driver and Lady Mountbatten. She seemed a very pleasant woman and wore Red Cross uniform. She looked tired and worn. Eventually, Lieutenant Colonel Lilly arrived with six or seven officers. He found me and said that he had been sent to take over the camp and evacuate the men. However, having seen the camp, he considered it would be an insult to me and those other WOs who had been in charge to do so. He asked if we would continue to run the camp and evacuate the men, which we did.

I had been told in advance that Lieutenant Colonel Lilly and other officers were coming. So, we took over the Jap guard hut which was the best and largest in the camp for their accommodation. Lieutenant Colonel Lilly was an inveterate smoker and we had an Australian who was a wizard at making cigarettes, so we managed to get some local tobacco, also some paper and made at least 500 very good cigarettes which we presented to the CO on his arrival. We also recruited his old batman to watch over him. I might add that Lieutenant Colonel Lilly had been given a very tough time at the hands of the *Kempeitai* [Japanese secret military police] and we had a lot of sympathy for him.

After a few hours in the camp, Lieutenant Colonel Lilly came to me in an angry state. He said 'When I left you, I asked if you would keep an eye on Sergeant Baker. You allowed him to go on a railway repair party and he is now in a poor state of health. Why?' I explained that many of our men were sick and when a repair party was called for I tried to send the fittest men. I left Sergeant Baker out and I was faced with sending a Corporal Warren who suffered from chronic malaria and for whom I had found a little job in the camp where he could keep out of the sun. [Corporal Albert Edward Warren (4756233) was in the same company as Eric (HQ). He was a married man from E17, London and was one of those who joined the 1/5 in June 1940 after their losses in France. He survived and returned home in 1945.] The MO had told me that if Corporal Warren left the Camp on such an enterprise, he would die. So, I had no alternative but to send Sergeant Baker. The CO would not accept this and I don't think he ever forgave me. What the relationship between those two was I was never to know. Sergeant Baker belonged to the 148th Field Regiment Royal Artillery and I suppose was rather a handsome fellow. [There was only one Sergeant Baker in the 148th Field Regiment Royal Artillery who was recorded as being taken prisoner on 15/02/42 at Singapore: Lance Sergeant Aubrey Arthur Bertram Baker 903873. He was in Tarsao and Tamuan as the same time as Eric and Lieutenant Colonel Lilly. Beyond Eric's comments, the reason for Lieutenant Colonel Lilly's concern for Lance Sergeant Baker is unknown.]

Later, whilst at Pratchai, the CO invited me and a few of my colleagues to an evening meal he had arranged for in the village. We took a Jap truck and went down to the village where on the upper floor of a café place, a meal table had been set out. We had a very good meal, a variety of all sorts of food, savoury, sweet and sour, backed by rice and accompanied by an endless supply of rice spirit. As the evening went on, all the men slipped under the table except the CO and I. The CO looked at me across the table and said 'Well, Roberts, I think we had better get them back to camp.' The following day I was late getting up and I had a terrible headache; needless to say, I had no more rice spirit.

The officers Lieutenant Colonel Lilly had brought with him to take over the camp were ignored and just lay on their beds. They were not pleased and submitted an adverse report on Lieutenant

Colonel Lilly but I don't suppose anything came of it. However, all the officers left the camp. I eventually left in the final party of thirty on a Jap lorry and the camp was handed over to the Dutch for whom no arrangements for evacuation had then been made. I remember as we drove through the camp gates, the Jap Officer who had been Camp Commandant was there and he gave me a rather embarrassed salute as we left. He was rather a rarity and had been as good as conditions would permit. Later a report in his favour was submitted to the Japanese War Crimes Trials Court at Singapore. [According to Pavillard (1962), this was Captain Suzuki.]

Siam
9 September 1945

My Darling,
I have already written to aunt so you will know the news, nothing of any note has occurred since then except a visit paid to the camp by Lady Louis Mountbatten today, not a very pleasant job for a woman. Anyhow, we all did our best to look as smart and civilized as possible. Afterwards, of course, we all made a dash to take our shirts off, a garment to which we have not yet become fully accustomed.

Quite a lot of our fellows have already been moved and I think this camp should be cleared in about another week. I am part of a nucleus which will be stopping until last, so naturally I am anxious for the move to be carried out at all speed in order that I can go to Rangoon. Movements after then will depend upon the availability of shipping.

Once we are 'out', I think we should be able to establish some sort of regular communication with home and then over the course of a few letters I may be able to give you a bit of history. At present I am doing my best to forget my shady past and am having no difficulty in doing so. The human memory is very short and one is finding that outstanding incidents are now slightly amusing.

It is certainly better so or one's future would be <u>entirely</u> dominated by the past. Actually, on the 16th of last month when we discovered we were no longer prisoners there was great enthusiasm but about three days later a reaction set in. I had a mild attack and it certainly is a peculiar sickness and one which the layman would hardly credit. I experienced the same thing in France and *on Singapore Island. It is of course the result of mental tension, but later one becomes adjusted to the changed conditions and one has no further trouble.*

Whilst I have not been without news of you for the last two and a half years, such news has been invariably out of date. I do hope you have been getting along well and none the worse for wartime conditions. I know you will give me all the information when you write. You should have a far more interesting autobiography than I but I don't suppose we shall really be able to compare notes until I get home.

Jim Parker is getting along well, so I hear, although I haven't seen him since July 1943 and as things are at present may not see him again until we are back.

Whilst the Officers were taken away from the ORs at the beginning of the year, our own CO is now back again and I hope that he and about 60 of my own unit will be able to return to England together. I have a great respect for the Colonel; he has done a fine job of work and has proved himself to be a man in all respects. The life we have led has been a searching test, but at all times he has had the men at the back of him which has at times proved to be a useful weapon against the Japs, whilst we were living in the jungle at any rate.

I cannot envisage the getting together of my own unit, or the remnants thereof, which is a thing I regret, because they have become split up.

Everyone says 'we shall be home for Christmas'; so here's hoping.

My kind regards to you, Father and all at home
Yours with all my love,
<u>*Eric*</u>

During the whole of the period between October 1941 and October 1945 Eunice wrote to me on a regular basis although I was unable to reply until August 1945 when the Jap war came to an end and I was able to write to her my first letter from Pratchai. Quite recently, I was told that Eunice wrote to a friend and said 'Hoorah: I've had a letter from Eric, there will be wedding bells by the end of next year.'

Chapter 20

August–November 1945

My little party of thirty duly arrived at Bangkok where we were quartered at the University. After a couple of days there we went by lorry to Bangkok airport, a small civilian one. After a wait, a Dakota came in and a flight lieutenant from it said to me 'We are running late, get your fellows on quickly, there are no landing lights at Rangoon.' My little party of thirty got on and sat down where we could, mostly on the floor, when the Flight Lieutenant said 'It's no good sitting there, come up forward and stand behind the pilot, otherwise we shall never get off.' We duly did that and the next thing I knew was that we had run off the landing strip into the mud. 'That's it,' said the Flight Lieutenant, 'we shall have to stay the night.' I objected at that stage and said 'We have thirty fellows here and if we can't get this thing back onto the runway it is a pity.' The Flight Lieutenant relented and we manhandled the plane back onto the runway. We were soon off and up to 20,000' to get over the mountains which separate Burma from Thailand. We were all shivering violently; there were a few blankets which we wrapped around us but that didn't help much. However, we dropped down and flew over the sea; in fact we were so low that I could see the flying fish jumping out of the water.

In due time I heard a voice from the front saying 'We are there.' I looked out and saw a small clearing in the jungle which seemed to be no bigger than a postage stamp. I closed my eyes and waited. Eventually it felt that the plane was running over corrugated sheeting and it came to a stop, the engines were shut off and we waited in silence. After a little time an RAF lorry emerged from the surrounding jungle, we all got on and were taken to an RAF Mess where we were given some food before being transported to Rangoon where we were quartered in a military hospital. There were comfortable beds with mosquito nets and the nurses there were members of Queen Alexandra's Imperial Military Nursing Service (QAIMNS). As I sat on the edge of my bed, there apparently being nothing else to do, one of the nurses coming by said to me 'I think you could do with a bottle of beer.' She went away and brought me a bottle of Whitbread's Pale Ale. The following day there were a few medical checks and we went by truck nearer to Rangoon where a very large tented camp had been established to receive ex-PoWs and internees, known as a Repatriation of All Prisoners of War and Internees (or RAPWI).

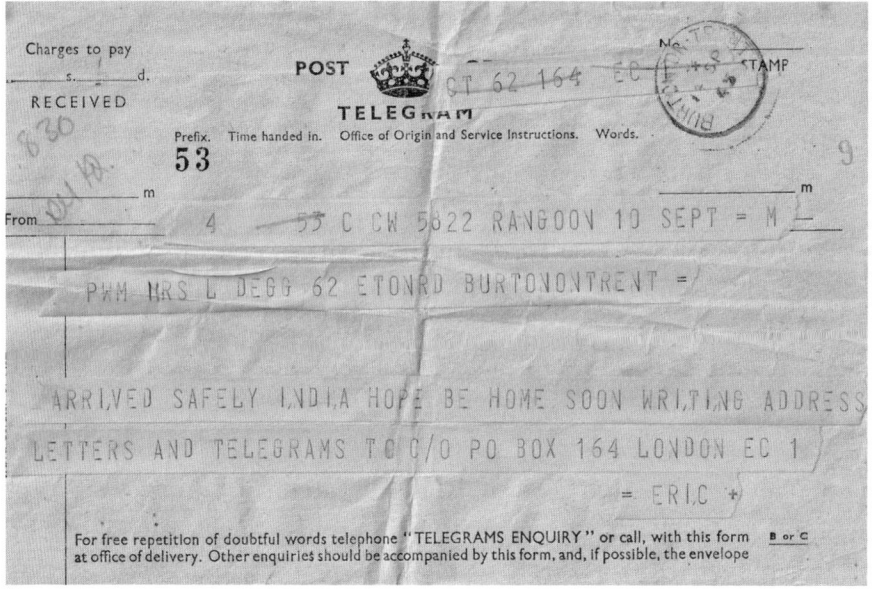

Telegram sent by Eric, September 1945.

> *Recovered PoW*
> *C/o P.O. Box 164*
> *London EC1*
> *9 September 1945*
>
> <u>*Darling,*</u>
> *Arrived here, Rangoon, yesterday from Bangkok, a journey which took about 3 hrs by air. I am actually in a British Base Hospital, and although not a patient, we are all treated similarly. There are our own nursing sisters here*

(these particular ones left England last month) and are the first European women we have seen (except one or two internees at Bangkok) since being taken prisoner. We had always regarded ourselves as 'white', but alongside these nurses, we look almost native. Anyhow, it is good to have a breath of civilisation once more.

We are back on a normal army diet and extremely glad to be off native food, although the latter if cooked properly by a local can be quite palatable and perhaps their standard of cooking is better than our own.

For the first time in my army career, am not part of the administration, and am in hospital. I must say that complete lack of responsibility is not to my liking, one has come to accept such things as one's due, but probably the rest will do me good. May land a job on the way home if by then I haven't cultivated a habit of complete inactivity which this spot, excellent as it is, may have created.

Unfortunately our Colonel has had to stay in Bangkok on this War Criminal stunt, so may not see him again until we get back.

Haven't had any mail from home yet, but maybe there is some at the Army Post Office in the town – will have a walk down in the morning to see, some of the fellows have managed to raise some.

There are a couple of improvised cinemas in the area, went to a show this afternoon, American films, beats me what has happened to the British films. Saw a film show in Bangkok, also American.

Last I heard of Jim was at Petchburi a fortnight or so ago but he is probably away by now. I have perhaps told you this before, having written to you all.

Everyone since things 'wrapped up' has been extremely kind, but shall be very glad to get rid of this damned tag 'Ex-PoW', inevitable but shall be pleased to be regarded as any ordinary troop, for to be quite honest I see nothing to make a song about.

Should be on the way home soon.

All my love
<u>*Eric*</u>

C/o P.O. Box 164
London EC1
9 September 1945

My Dear Aunt,

Am now out of Siam, for which many thanks. Arrived here (Rangoon) yesterday by air. Organisation compared with the past is excellent. We were all admitted to hospital whether sick or otherwise. Incidentally I am not sick, but expect to be here for a few days.

Was able to stay a few days in Bangkok before coming away. This is quite a pleasant city in an Asiatic way. Some parts of it are quite modern with reinforced concrete buildings and good roads, but always nestling up to the better parts of the city are the squalid native buildings and conditions of the old town. A tram service runs until six o'clock in the evenings and from expenses a tram ride is the cheapest commodity in Bangkok. For example on the night before we left I was with a few other fellows in a café and eight bottles of beer were ordered, these amounting to $150. Considering the rate of exchange is about $170 to £5 sterling you can judge for yourself what fares are like.

I was quarantined for a few days at the university, which is in a good district, buildings in the immediate vicinity were the broadcasting station, Ministries for the Interior and Defence and the Royal Palace. The latter was open to visitors, but unfortunately was not able to look round it, having had to spend a couple of days at HQ. Bangkok has not been badly damaged by our bombing except the railway system, workshops etc. which have been well and truly cleaned up. Most of the large railway bridges have been destroyed which made things difficult under the old regime having to transship ammunition etc. and ferry it across rivers and so forth. Living with the enemy as we have done, there is no doubt that they have been beaten.

All there is to be done here at present is to eat, smoke and rest. I am afraid a continuation of this will not be very palatable having led an active life free from enforced inactivity due to sickness.

We are lucky to have British nursing sisters here, very welcome after seeing no European women for so many years. Although it is rather a strain, for one's conversation has become not of the best and one has to go warily and avoid 'armyness'.

There is plenty to read here, and everyone is busily engaged in catching up. Particularly in relation to the news.

Will be very glad to hear the latest news from you all, have had no mail yet but expect to shortly.

All the best
Lots of love
Eric

We settled down in the camp which was quite comfortable and there was no shortage of food. Whilst we were there an Entertainments National Service Association (ENSA) concert party put on a show. I was very sorry for the young women in it who were obviously distressed by the climate; however, they did their best and we enjoyed their show. Whilst in that camp, I walked down the main road towards Rangoon proper. The road was lined with all manner of earth-moving equipment for airfield construction. I had never seen such an assembly. I suppose most of it was of USA origin. By now I felt a free man; I had lost my responsibilities and decided I would take things easily.

> *Recovered Pw.*
> *C/o P.O. Box 164*
> *London EC1*
> *19 September 1945*
>
> *Darling,*
> *Received a letter from you today dated 28 August 1945. Glad you are liking your job, but why change? Possibly the answer is in a previous letter.*
> *Am at present in a transit camp awaiting embarkation, when, it seems doubtful. There are quite a number of my own Battalion in this camp and we had hoped to go home together, but the confusion caused in sorting them out would appear to make it impracticable.*
> *At present we are all unemployed and consequently anxious to get moving. Previously being busy and having no time for thought it didn't seem to be of prime import. Queer, you know, being out here seems to have become one's life, although after seeing you again I shall have changed my mind.*
> *You had better get a plan of campaign ready (not too many relatives) for I shall be having six weeks' leave to kill when I return. How I shall be able to occupy myself for six weeks beats me, no offence.*
> *You will have to give me a resume on this Land Army business. All I can remember of them is a collection of rather unattractive females in breeches which don't suit them but I'm hoping you have improved the standard.*
> *As for a lilt in the voice having lived with so many cockneys for so long, you will probably find I speak like one. You will be able to decide for yourself at Kineton 135, which will be my first job on landing. I am reminded of a similar*

> instance at Sheffield, five years ago, seems like ten. A period I would not care to live again.
>
> How has all your family been faring? Have had no news of mine yet. This mail business is rather tricky with a floating population such as we are.
>
> Looking forward,
> Yours, with all my love.
> <u>Eric</u>

It was not long before a man from the camp office came and asked me to go with him. Arriving at the office I was told that I was to be a Draft Conducting Officer, that I would be given the names of thirty men who should be contacted. In due time I was to take them down to the dock and then see them safely conducted to the UK. So, I had responsibilities again. When I had my list of thirty men, I was faced with having to find them in a large tented camp with thousands of men but fortunately I saw that I had three Sergeants. So, I found my three Sergeants, gave them each a list of nine men for whom they were to be responsible, told them to find them and I also told them where to find me. I returned to my tent and in time had instructions to get my thirty men down to the docks. They were all assembled and we went down to the docks in a truck. There was quite a lot of sunken shipping in the dock but I found a tank landing craft which was doing a bit of ferrying. This took us out to HMS *Chitral* which was lying some distance off. The landing craft arrived at a companionway at the side of the ship. I was the first up and was greeted at the top by the Ship's Regimental Sergeant Major with outstretched hand. He had been with my Battalion but had been transferred elsewhere about four and a half years earlier. He said 'This ship is dry, be in my cabin at 6.30 this evening.' I was allocated quite a good cabin with four other WOs and we had a steward to keep things tidy. There was also a WOs' Mess, where we were well treated. Soon we set off and that night I went to the Ship's Regimental Sergeant Major's cabin to find several gathered there with plenty of gin, followed by the evening meal. It was something I didn't care for and so I gave up the gin session.

Colombo
6 October 45

My Dear Aunt,
Left Rangoon on the 1st and should be home by the end of the month. I do hope you are receiving my mail, have not heard from you since the conclusion, but have had one letter from Eunice. There is actually no point in sending more mail out for the odds of getting it are very remote being on the move.

Everyone is enjoying this long looked forward to trip and most are having a complete rest. When we came aboard, I think the skipper expected sick men, but the majority are fit enough. There are of course quite a lot in hospitals at Rangoon which will remain there until I imagine either hospital ships take them off to India or they are well enough to travel in the ordinary way.

I shall soon have to be thinking about a job, which is rather a problem, but I am hoping to be 'back in' by the New Year. There will be a fair amount of leeway to be made good, but feel that opportunities should appear. After all, six years ago I was their king on terms of six months and I should have not been as anxious to get into the service and should have taken the opportunity of an extension.

Anyhow, probably it was for the best for I am at least alive and kicking, if having missed the better sides of war (if there is such a thing).

Have heard nothing whatever of Barbara and family; in the words of James Forsyte 'no one tells me anything' [reference to a character, Soames' father, from Galsworthy's *The Forsyte Saga*].

Keep the old chin up.

Love
<u>*Eric*</u>

There was a Matron on board, who came to me a day or so out and told me that there were beer and spirits aboard but we were dry because the Americans were. Why she came to me, I don't know but she enquired if I thought it would be a good idea if the men had some. I agreed and she said she would see the Captain. She was good as her word and that evening the bar was open in the WOs' Mess and in other places I suppose. The thirty men I was supposed to be in charge of were quartered in the hold in bunks and I went down to see them. One of the Sergeants said to me 'It is alright for you – plenty of booze.' I said 'I will see you get some' and went down to the galley for a bucket which I took to the WOs' Mess and had filled with beer. I suppose there would be at least two gallons and I took it down to the hold and a cheer went up. An interesting side issue about the Sergeant I gave the beer to was that during the night he felt sick, went up on deck but didn't make the rail. He returned to his bunk and at first light discovered he had lost his false teeth. He rushed on deck just in time to recover them before they were washed into the scuppers by those who were hosing down the deck. Later on there was a bar in the Men's Mess.

A few days out and I was in the WOs' Mess one day when the Chief Steward came to me and said that twenty or so of the Women's Royal Naval Service (WRNS, popularly known as Wrens) were coming aboard at Colombo. There was only the WO's Mess for them to be accommodated in and what should he do with them? The

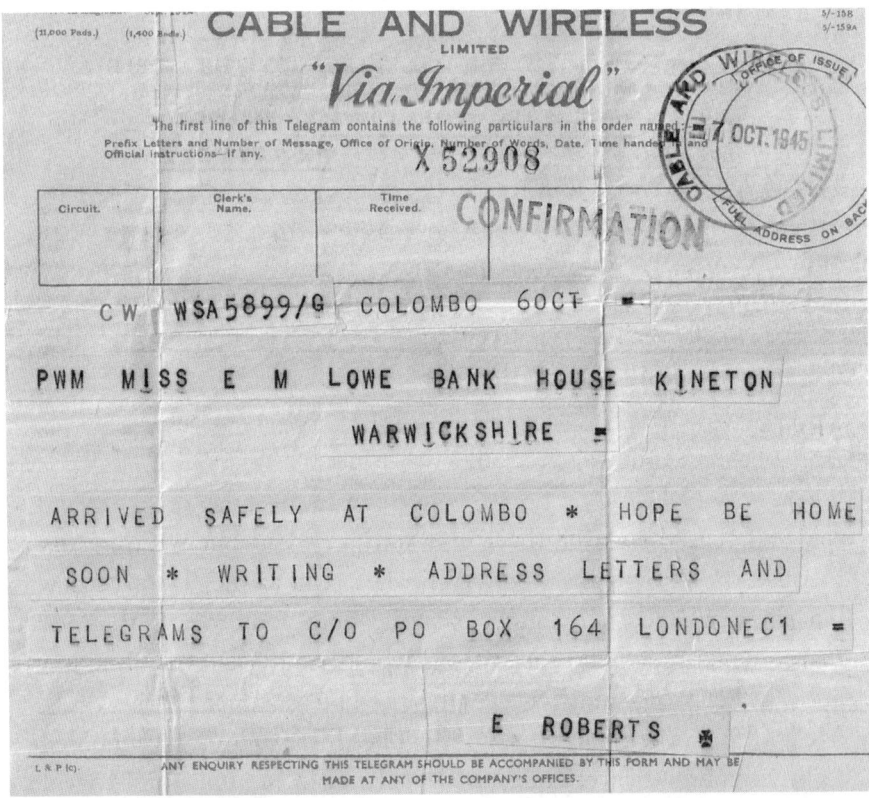

Telegram from Eric, October 1945.

Mess was quite large and I pointed to a number of tables at the end of the room which were not used. All he said was 'Bread and bread is no good.' [Cryptic, but meaning that males and females should be mixed and not separated.]

The following morning when I arrived in the Mess for breakfast, just a little late, I found that at a large table sat the WO members of the Mess and between each sat a very smart-looking Wren. Conversation to start with was a little slow but as the days went by things improved. Next to me was a very pleasant well-spoken girl and having been out of circulation for at least four years, I was very much out of touch with news and what had been happening generally. She talked to me at great length and helped me quite a bit. We had a little arrangement and before the evening meal met on deck and had two or three turns round whilst she talked.

Colombo
6 October 1945

My Darling,

I think the 30th of the month should do it. Certainly has been a long time but the end of the story should be perfectly orthodox.

Don't know whether we shall be able to get ashore or not yet, hope so, should make a pleasant break.

Left Rangoon on the 1st (or was it the 2nd?) and so far it has been a good trip, everyone having a much needed rest including your devoted.

I am afraid your affianced will shortly be transferring to the great army of unemployed, not a very pleasant prospect. I think I will probably stay in the Army and come out East again, on the other hand, perhaps I won't.

I think Jim must have gone home ahead of me, haven't seen anything of him at all although I know he was alright after the finish.
Yours
With all my love
Eric

HMS Chitral
14 October 1945

My Dear Aunt,

I am now about half way home, another fourteen days should find me in England. At present we are in the Red Sea which is proving to be the hottest part of the journey. I don't think it is really any hotter than we have been accustomed to but am inclined to think it is the diet which is of a more heating nature. Shall be glad when we get into the med. (sorry can't spell it) where it will be cooler.

We spent a couple of days at Colombo where we had a very fine reception from various members of the women's services who certainly did their best for us. The whole thing was very well organized indeed. Colombo is quite a pleasant spot and is an example of the civilisation we have missed so much. Incidentally, at Colombo they have had one air raid during the war.

Have heard nothing from you at all yet, in fact my intelligence of your doings is about twelve months old. We are hoping to get ashore at Port Suez where we shall get our warm clothing.

Give my kind regards to Ronald and everyone. Do hope you are keeping well, I am. Feeling fine and having quite a holiday.

Love
Eric

HMS Chitral
15 October 45

Darling,

Getting well on the way home, in fact have done about half of the journey. Should be at Port Suez tomorrow where we shall be able to get this mail away.

To date the trip has been a very pleasant one with quite a holiday spirit aboard. There are a number of WRENs messing with us which has to a great extent relieved the monotony of conversation. They came aboard at Colombo and so far as I know are all returning to England for demobilisation.

Actually I am quite at a loss to know what to write about, there is so much and yet so little. What of course is needed is something to reply to for it is rather like one person doing all the talking with neither a 'yes' nor a 'no' from the other which situation is quite impossible.

> *With me are about ninety of my old Battalion; quite a number have left on previous boats, but I am afraid we shall finish up with rather a shattering figure under 'losses'.*
>
> *We had a whist drive the other night, something which I had previously never attended, but we spent quite a pleasant evening, nobody taking the game seriously which was a good thing.*
>
> *Also one of the girls had a twenty-first birthday which we of course had to celebrate. Everyone did their bit and it was quite a success. Had it been a fellow, I doubt if so much interest would have been taken.*
>
> *Give my kind regards to all at home.*
>
> *All my love*
> <u>*Eric*</u>

We pushed on into the Red Sea and called at Aqaba in Jordan where we went ashore and were equipped with European clothing. Then through the Suez and into the Mediterranean, a brief stop off Gibraltar for mail, into the Atlantic and docking at Southampton.

Chapter 21

November 1945–1946: Return and Readjustment

The first ashore were the civilians aboard and the Wrens. I stood by the ship's rail looking at the proceedings on the dock when my friendly Wren came to me to say goodbye. She said she had enjoyed my company, surprisingly gave me a quick peck on the cheek and trotted off down the gangway into the arms of a young naval officer waiting on the dock.

Ashore we went to a transit camp and having delivered my thirty men, I was now a comparatively free agent. I took a trip around the camp, there was a Navy, Army and Air Force Institutes (NAAFI), a cinema and a Sergeants' Mess and my quarters were comfortable. That evening most of the men went out – they had seen too many American servicemen about with local girls on their arms and decided they must sort a few out. I didn't wish to be involved in that, had a bite to eat and went to the cinema. There was trouble in the town and I was glad not to be part of it.

Next day I was concerned with my pay and going on leave. In the process I was told that I was not properly dressed in that I was not wearing my medal ribbons! I very soon found that qualification for medals was a farce. The 1939/40 Star intended for the original BEF had been extended to the 1939/45 Star and those coming into the forces six months after the end of the war would qualify. This also applied to other campaign medals. Men who were in the UK at the end of the war and went out as occupation forces were given the Pacific and/or Burma Stars, being treated exactly as those who had fought during the whole of the campaign in that part of world. I said I suppose I am entitled to the Defence Medal (which had been given to ladies who had served tea to the forces in England) but was told I couldn't have that as I had not been in England long enough. I was disgusted by the whole business but a member of the Women's

Royal Voluntary Service (WRVS) sewed onto my tunic the ribbons of the 1939/45 Star, the Pacific Star and the War Medal. As soon as possible I went on leave to Burton-on-Trent and was attached to Branston Central Ordnance Depot for 'Pay and Rations'.

Eric told me that after being turned down for the Defence Medal, he then went to the NAAFI and saw the girl serving the tea wearing the Defence Medal ribbon, hence the comment. The combination of the 1939/45 Star, Pacific Star and War Medal usually indicates that the recipient was a Far East PoW. In general, the Defence Medal was awarded for three years' home service or six months' service in areas under air attack or closely threatened. Therefore, the absence of a Defence Medal indicates a significant amount of overseas service or curtailed service (for example, as a PoW). At the time, those captured in 1940 in France with A Company of the 1/5 Foresters or in Norway with the 8/Foresters received only two medals: the 1939/45 Star and the War Medal.

When I came back to England and on leave, Eunice was then a warden at a land army hostel in Kineton. I went to Kineton once or twice and stayed with Eunice's friends in the village. Eunice had managed to get Kate at the same place in the capacity of cook. When Eunice knew she was leaving Kineton, she was concerned about Kate and set out to find her a husband. Eunice was a great organiser and things usually worked out. I can vouch for that.

Although my copy of the report on Japanese war atrocities had been lost at Tamuan in 1944, it emerged that one copy was later brought back to the UK, I think by Major Barnett. A report was submitted from the Drill Hall at Derby to the Singapore War Crimes Trials. I believe I typed this in which evidence was given against a number of Japs; at the same time a few Japs were recommended for clemency. [This was Major F.W. (Jack) Barnett (41413), 1/5 Foresters. He suffered severe wounds prior to capture at Singapore and was sent to a PoW camp on the Japanese mainland at Tajiri. Despite this, he survived and was repatriated in 1945.]

For three and a half years, I was the recipient of information about Foresters (and others) and took any opportunity to question men. Of course, I kept a record of all deaths in camps where we exercised any authority. This recording continued at Tamuan, where there was an opportunity to question a lot of men from various camps. At Tamuan a clerk in the camp office, Bombardier Wells, Royal Artillery, who wrote a good hand was given the job of writing a consolidated record of all deaths on the railway, so far as it was possible. [There was no one of this rank at Tamuan. The surname may be incorrect. Unfortunately, this man cannot be positively identified.] Somehow, two stiff covered record books were made for this purpose and when completed I had one of these with other information (records of the camps we were in, nominal rolls, deaths and burials and a map of the railways I obtained in Rangoon).

I brought these records back with me from Pratchai, Thailand to the UK. Back in England and on leave, Lieutenant Colonel Lilly and a few other members of the original 1/5 Foresters re-established themselves in the old TA Drill Hall in Derby. The Battalion had an Honorary Colonel (Kerr) who had taken an interest in the Battalion during the war – he turned up at the Drill Hall and there was also a part-time female clerk. [Honorary Colonel John Daniel Kerr MC, TD was a career officer, having been commissioned into the Sherwood Foresters prior to the First World War. Lieutenant Colonel Lilly succeeded him as Honorary Colonel in 1949.] So far as I know, the Drill Hall Office was open three half-days a week and I turned up at these times for several months until the early part of 1946. The Office may have been open at other times but these were irregular and I had no key to the office. I took my records there and set about sorting out the affairs of the Battalion. As I wrote earlier, the Battalion set off in 1941 with a total of 1001 Officers and ORs and one of these absented himself in Halifax, Nova Scotia, leaving a total of 1000 which were eventually disembarked at Singapore on 31 January 1942. Numerous people came to see me at the Drill Hall with information, some items were new to me and others either confirmed or contradicted the records I already had. I persevered until I thought I had exhausted all sources of information. Information was transmitted to Infantry Records, York, the War Office, the War Graves Commission and other organisations who may have been involved. There were also, of course, relatives of the deceased – this was particularly a very sad business. There were other matters to deal with such as men's pay and allowances.

After a time the Battalion was given a Civic Reception in Derby. A parade was held in the Old Market Square in Derby where a platform had been erected upon which sat local dignitaries including the Mayor of Derby [Alderman T. Johnson] and the Duke of Devonshire [Lieutenant Colonel Edward William Spenser Cavendish KG, MBE, TD of the 24th Derbyshire Yeomanry]. The Mayor made a very stumbling speech and when he sat down, had fallen 'aitches' been tangible, he would have been up to the knees in them. I was standing in the front rank and the Duke was obviously embarrassed during the Mayor's speech, continually crossing and uncrossing his legs. So far as I can remember, of the 1000 Officers and ORs of the Battalion landed at Singapore, we were able to muster the residue of approximately 400, the rest being casualties.

Having done as much as I could at the Drill Hall, Derby, and extracted all the information I could from my records, I went to collect my records from the box where I had kept them in the Drill Hall Office. My records had gone. I questioned those who had been visiting the office during the period, Colonel Kerr, Lieutenant Colonel Lilly, Captain Coxon and others, but none would admit to knowing anything about the papers. Knowing Coxon, I suspected him at the time. Many years later Wilf Wood said that he had seen records in the possession of Aspdin which he thought were in my writing. [Captain Geoffrey Slater Aspdin (75998) was with the Motor Transport section of the 1/5. He later commanded the 1/5 from 1956 to 1958 and became an Honorary Colonel.] I raised the matter with Aspdin, who became most indignant (Coxon had died in the meantime). In 1986 Wilf Wood, speaking on Aspdin's behalf, said that a Colonel connected with the Sherwood Forester-Worcestershire Regiment had come by records which he thought were related to our old Battalion and could they be verified. At about that time Nicklin had also died. I said I would do what I could if I had sight of them. I have heard nothing since but the whole matter was very odd. I later discovered that Nicklin and Coxon were close friends; they had joined the Regiment as boys in the band and apparently soldiered together during the whole of their army careers.

George White noted that

> Eric put an enormous amount of work into recording the details of members of the 1/5 Foresters taken prisoners of the Japanese at Singapore in 1942. I knew that his records disappeared from the Drill Hall in 1946 and that this was a major blow to him, especially in view of the great amount of work he had put in in maintaining them, given the great and ever present risk of holding that information whilst in the PoW camps. He never told me, so far as I can remember, that he was holding these records. Eric well knew the risk of holding any records etc. I provided an example at Wampo on the occasion of the first unannounced search. I had a few pages written from various books describing Cape Town and Malaya (kept in innocent expectation as a record on my return home). One of them bore the pencil drawing of a map of Malaya about 1½ inches long. It was found in my kit and it took about 30 minutes before a *Kempeitai* Sergeant to convince him that it was not being kept for escape purposes. On its return the pages were rapidly deposited in the latrine.

I never did find the records but on occasion heard rumours of their possible whereabouts. This was another illustration of the TA attitude towards me. After my work was done at the Drill Hall and I had stopped going there, I received the final indignity from the TA members: a letter to me from Lieutenant Colonel Lilly thanking me for all the work I had done for the Battalion and enclosing £10 for my trouble. For many months I had travelled three times a week to Derby by train at my own expense and given my time freely. During this time the old TA members who might have assisted were conspicuous by their absence.

I was still on extended leave and was eventually called to Birmingham for a medical examination at an office near to Birmingham, New Street Station. I met an old Doctor who didn't seem to have a clue and was passed fit for discharge. Later I went to a depot at Hereford where I was eventually issued with my demobilisation clothing: a felt hat, suit, shoes, shirt and other small items, plus a raincoat.

That was it. I was later issued with a post office savings account book into which had been paid my accumulated earnings. I think this also included a small gratuity, so ended nearly seven years' military service, an abortive effort conducted by those who could only be described as criminal idiots. I was of the opinion in 1946 that there should have been War Crimes Trials in the UK and fifty years on I am still of that opinion.

In 1946 I was coming up to my twenty-eighth year. I considered staying on in the Army but peacetime soldiering did not appeal to me. Some of my friends were considering getting off to colleges and universities. I considered other work or going back to my old job. I felt that I just wished to settle down quietly, marry and have a home with Eunice. Eunice was in agreement with this and that was what I did.

Eunice and I married in September 1946 and for a month or two we lived with Aunt until we bought the house in Sydney Street; from there we moved with our sons, Jim and Chris, to Lodge Hill. However, our early married life was a bit of a struggle, we were usually short of money but we both worked together and Eunice bore up remarkably well. It could have not been easy for her but she never complained. I was happy and Eunice never said she wasn't. My very happy married life with Eunice and our two sons, James and Christopher, also my working life to retirement in 1984 are all another story.

George and Eric were indeed fortunate. Of the 1,001 men who arrived in the Far East with the 1/5 Sherwood Foresters, 61 were killed at Singapore, 95 drowned while being transported as PoWs by the Japanese and 203 died of disease and neglect in the camps. Total losses were 359 (Housley, 1995). The surviving 642 men continued to fight ill-health and untreated post-traumatic stress disorder for the rest of their lives. Their efforts were eclipsed by the more successful campaigns of the later war years and they were often charged with 'not fighting' or simply 'surrendering'.

Chapter 22

Epilogue

When Eric died in 2001, a Union Flag was placed on his coffin. Under very different circumstances it had been used for many funerals in the past, and this was its last. Eric had given the flag to the Sherwood Foresters' Museum in 1965 and Eric's son Chris arranged for it to be borrowed for Eric's funeral.

The two letters below describe how this flag was found, concealed and used. The letters are in contrast to Mrs Robinson's account in the Appendix, which states that the flag was 'torn up', although there may have been more than one flag.

> <u>Sherwood Foresters Museum</u>
>
> 7 April 1965
>
> It occurs to me that the Union Jack herewith may be of some interest, if not now, possibly in the years to come.
>
> Briefly, following the fall of Singapore to the Japanese in February 1942, a party of British prisoners under the Japanese was removing some of the contents of Government House, Singapore. Documents and other items left behind by the British were being thrown from the windows and burnt on fires in the grounds. Being burnt were a number of flags; one of these flags, the Union Jack herewith, was taken by Corporal Halfside, 1/5th Battalion The Sherwood Foresters, concealed about his body beneath his shirt and brought back to a PoW Camp in River Valley Road, Singapore.
>
> Later in 1942, Corporal Halfside, with others of the same Battalion, was moved by the Japanese into Siam for work on a military railway to be built to link Bangkok with Rangoon. During the building of this railway, many of Corporal Halfside's comrades died and the flag was almost invariably used for the simple committals conducted in the jungle. The Japanese were rarely, if ever, present at these burials.

The Japanese had a strong objection to flags or anything of a nationalistic character, other than their own, and had the flag been discovered by the Japanese during their various searches of prisoners' belongings, it would most certainly have been destroyed and Corporal Halfside would undoubtedly have received a severe beating.

Corporal Halfside carried the flag from place to place in the jungle for some time until he and others were shipped by the Japanese to Japan. At this stage, retaining the flag was unwise for Corporal Halfside and he handed it to his CO, Lieutenant Colonel H.H. Lilly, who kept it until the early part of 1945, during which time it continued to be used for burials.

Early in 1945, Colonel Lilly, then in Tamuan, Siam, and other Officers were separated from the Other Ranks. Rather than lose the flag at that stage, Colonel Lilly entrusted it to the writer. As necessity arose, the flag continued to be used, but with the knowledge of Japanese reverses conditions became more difficult. For concealment, the flag was sewn into a small bag made from a piece of rice sack and this used as a pillow. Movement from camp to camp involved searches by the Japanese and to avoid discovery and loss of the flag during movement, it was concealed amongst the Japanese's own baggage, being recovered at the end of the journey.

When the knowledge of the Japanese defeat became known in August 1945, this flag was flown above a PoW Camp at Pratchai, some 60 miles from Bangkok. The flag was brought back to England in October of the same year.

4978071 Sergeant E.B. Roberts
1/5th Battalion, The Sherwood Foresters

Corporal E. Halfside (4981054) was a married man and was in HQ Company with Eric. He was one of the fortunate ones to survive the sinking of the *Rakuyo Maru* and the *Kachidoki Maru*. He returned to home in Hertfordshire in 1944 (Housley, 1995).

> REGIMENTAL HEADQUARTERS
> THE SHERWOOD FORESTERS
> (NOTTINGHAM AND DERBYSHIRE REGIMENT)
> Triumph Road, Lenton, Nottingham
> *Telephone: Nottingham 75516*
>
> *Please address any reply to*
> REGIMENTAL SECRETARY
> *And quote:* SF/132   14 April 1965
>
> Dear *Mr Roberts*
>   I think the Union Jack together with its story is a most interesting exhibit. Even more impressive than the feat of keeping the flag hidden throughout the years is the spirit behind it. Throughout that period of suffering and degradation in Jap hands some people still considered that having one's own flag was important, just shows how the Japs failed to break the spirit of the PoW.
>   A worthy exhibit of courage and defiance in adversity.
>   On behalf of the Regiment, thank you.
>
>   Yours sincerely,
>   Lieutenant Colonel
>   Regimental Secretary
>   (G.P. GOFTON-SALMOND)

George White died in 2012; however, I shall leave the closing words to him:

> So one could go on and on; suffice it to say that I was one of the lucky ones. My proposed accountancy course saved me because I never worked on the railway. At all the railway camps, I was involved in keeping some records of the 'Jap pay' for each individual and in running in effect canteen supplies for purchase of eggs, bundles of tobacco and anything else the CO managed to buy off the Thai sampans with Jap permission. I wonder if Eric had a hand in ensuring I remained in effect the 'PRI Clerk'. Eric carried out his military duties in an exemplary manner and we couldn't have had a better battalion 'Clerk'. I remember him with great admiration for the way he did

the job and his cheerfulness when things were bad. As you say, he will be missed. He was my last link with those PoW days and the contact from time to time over the years has kept our memories alive. I hope as far as Eric was concerned that I did not cause him to remember too many bad times; he usually reminded me of amusing incidents, like pouring water over me at Tonchan when malaria was so bad that I didn't get washed too often! Lastly I do hope this narrative fills in some of the years which it seems he didn't talk about. With grateful memories of Eric, from George White.

Appendix

Mrs Robinson's Account of PoW Life

Following the repatriation of some of the PoWs after the sinking of the *Rakuyo Maru* and the *Kachidoki Maru*, Mrs Hope Robinson worked with two of these former PoWs to produce an account of life in the camps. Mrs Hope Robinson was the wife of Major Paul Maltby Robinson (38749). Major 'Maltby' Robinson was credited with bringing the 1/5 back from France in June 1940 and was captured at Singapore. Despite being wounded in February 1942, he survived and returned home in 1945.

The two men came from No. 4 Group, where Eric was still being held. It was presented as an accurate account from reliable eye-witnesses; however, it omits details of the true horrors of the camps and of the conduct of the guards and commandants. There are likely to have been two main reasons for this. Firstly, the War Office had instructed former PoWs not to disclose information about their experiences. Secondly, and more importantly, there was a strong desire in most of the PoWs to spare their relatives the full details and thus protect them from the truth.

Articles from the local news confirm how 'reassuring' the account was to the PoWs' families. The report shown also includes confirmation by the Red Cross of its accuracy, despite the fact that no Red Cross officials had visited the camps; a fact stated in the letters to Eunice from the Red Cross themselves. Because of the contents of the report and the credence given to it, there was a gulf between the view of the camps from the Home Front and the reality experienced by the PoWs. In the majority of cases this information gap was never bridged. Returning men never spoke of these things to their families or friends. For the most part their experiences would never be retold. In any case, for those at home the treatment of Allied PoWs by the Japanese was beyond comprehension.

The report gives sole credit for management and organization of the camp to the officers and there is no recognition given to any ORs. However, as the production and distribution of the account was led by the wife of an officer, this is perhaps unsurprising.

The report is reproduced in full below and was, at the time, provided to anyone who requested it:

From Mrs. Hope Robinson, ILKESTON, Derbyshire   29.11.44

The following details of life as a Prisoner of War in Thailand have been collected by Mrs P.M. Robinson, wife of Major Robinson, 1/5th Battalion Sherwood Foresters, now in No. 4 Camp from two men recently returned from this camp:

Private Ward, 1/5 Sherwood Foresters and Gunner Simpson Royal Artillery left Thailand at the end of August. They were being transferred with a number of labour units to work in Japan as the work of road-making on which they had been engaged in Thailand had been completed. On arrival in Singapore they found the island had been stripped of its food and all articles of value and comfort by the Japanese troops. Nothing seemed to have been left unspoiled.

They sailed from Singapore on 6 September and on 12 September at 4 am were torpedoed by U.S. submarines. Although unable to swim Private Ward was in the water until 6 pm on 15 September. Some were picked up only on the fifth day. After torpedoing, the Japanese crew and guards took to the life-boats. The British were able to improvise a certain number of rafts by lashing together some of the hatches and most had life-belts of a sort, although many of these proved ineffective. No food or water was available until they were rescued and many were unable to survive the terrible ordeal. They were landed at Saipan and taken to Hospital and on 1 October sailed for the States by way of the Marshall Islands and Hawaii, reaching San Francisco on 23 October. They crossed America to New York, arriving home on 15 November. Their welcome in America and the wonderful help and hospitality they received impressed them greatly.

Private Ward and Gunner Simpson both looked in excellent health. They appeared to be in excellent spirits and did not seem to be suffering from any mental strain or reaction. They both said they had regained a certain amount of weight on the journey home but neither had lost an undue amount while Prisoners of War. Their relatives said they seemed only slightly thinner and in no other way altered. Both said that they already felt quite used to their freedom but were not yet quite used to

British food and certainly not to the amazingly luxurious dishes they had been treated to in the States.

Three months after the fall of Singapore the troops moved to Thailand. No. 4 Camp really consists of four different parts and was made up of several thousands of men. The groups moved about frequently according to the work they were required to do. At first the Japanese put great pressure on both men and officers to make roads through the jungle. This was when most of the 'savage' treatment referred to in the press was inflicted. As the work got under way the officers ceased work, much to the relief of the other ranks who did not like to see them under the discipline of the Japanese guards. Some stayed in the jungle to look after the men, including a number of Royal Army Medical Corps Officers, others were moved to the rest camps. Conditions began to be much improved. No. 4 Camp was established around the Bangkok area and men were sent there for hospital treatment and to rest and recuperate. The Camp was moved several times as work on the roads progressed. When the men left Thailand No. 4 Camp was near to Bangpong [*sic*] and conditions were very satisfactory, and the following details refer to life in this camp. Gardens were dug and vegetables were beginning to grow and a certain number of cattle were being kept.

Punishment was meted out to workers for three main offences, not working hard enough (often through the effects of malaria) or for talking or smoking while working, and took the form of beating with stout bamboo rods. As the pressure of work decreased so did the punishment and so long as a man did his best he was left unmolested. Naturally, some men resented the discipline and by showing their independence or by insulting the guards asked for trouble, but most had the good sense to adapt themselves to circumstance and comforted themselves by only inwardly despising their captors. Owing to the size of the Camp and the way it was divided up, it is not easy for the escaped men to give details of all the members in the Camp. In effect the men only knew intimately those who were in their individual labour group, although they know many others by sight if shown a photograph but cannot remember them by name.

Situation: Nearest town was Bangpong [*sic*]. Camp situated on a river which was the only source of water available for drinking and washing. All drinking supplies had to be boiled and although bathing was allowed at some seasons, during the cholera season even washing water had to be boiled, and cooking utensils had to be boiled, also knives, forks, etc.

Climate: Very hot indeed. Rain at certain seasons when flooding occurred. Nights were sometimes cold, but always hot in daytime.

Health: Malaria very general, chiefly the type known as B2, which is least serious, but recurs every three or four weeks. Most men went down regularly with attacks. For a short while at the beginning, quinine was not available in sufficient quantity and the situation was serious and a number of patients died. Lately plentiful supplies were available and could be bought and the situation was improving. Dysentery was also common and some cholera, although no serious epidemics through the Camp. All men were strongly tanned, and except when down with malaria, looked quite fit. Nearly all had more or less accustomed themselves to the climate and did not feel undue discomfort. Hospital arrangements were admirably run by the R.A.M.C. and endless trouble was taken to ensure patients the maximum attention and comfort. The attitude of the doctors who went into the jungle with the working parties was much admired. Many of these did not hesitate to insist on sending sick men down to the rest camps despite the Japanese guards who tried to prevent them. By their determination they succeeded in their decision, thereby considerably easing the men's plight.

Camp Discipline: Colonel Lilly of the 1/5th Sherwood Foresters was in charge of all troops in No. 4 Camp. Any complaints of treatment were made to him and he referred them to the Japanese Commandant. Private Ward and Gunner Simpson could not speak too highly of all that Colonel Lilly did for the welfare of the men. At first the Japanese tried to prevent the men from singing at work. The Commandant asked Colonel Lilly how it was that men who were prisoners and who were certain to be defeated could possibly wish to sing. Colonel Lilly told him that no one would be able to make them believe this and nothing could stop them from singing. After this, all attempts to prevent them were given up and the men say they found singing a great help in keeping up their spirits.

Camp Administration: This was carried out entirely by the Officers. They were left to organise camp life as they thought best. As the men were working out of the Camp the Officers were mainly responsible for maintaining the Camp itself, keeping it clean, digging latrines etc. Officers of each battalion lived in their own quarters. The Foresters, for example, built themselves a very nice hut where they all slept together. Officers were responsible for making the gardens and for running the canteen which was in Major Barnett's charge. The men were paid only a miserable wage. Ten days' pay would buy ten cigarettes. The Officers therefore put aside almost the whole of their pay to buy supplementary food for the whole camp and drugs for the hospital. Had it not been for this money, the men could not have survived. Parties of Officers were allowed to go down to Bangpong [sic] on shopping expeditions for supplies of food, drugs and tobacco. No intoxicating liquors could be had, although some men tried to brew their own from rice, without any very successful results. Occasionally, supplies could be got by bribing the guards but not as a general rule or in any quantity.

Food: Staple diet was rice. Each man got one pint per meal. Although at first unpalatable, everyone soon became used to this food. Although sufficient in camp when supplemented, this amount was barely sufficient while the men were working. They therefore collected various edible roots and leaves from the jungle which they named 'watercress', 'spinach', etc. In Camp vegetables could be got and small supplies of dried salt fish. Bananas, mangoes and yams were in abundance and other fruits. The cooks became adept at making various dishes out of the few available ingredients. For example, a form of pastry became very popular made from crushed rice and yam flour. This allowance of food could not be called really inadequate because the general state of health was satisfactory. To say the least, it was monotonous but bearable. Tobacco could be bought, chiefly the black native variety which the men rolled in whatever bits of paper they could scrounge.

Recreation: All books which were salvaged from Singapore were collected by the Officers and made into a library. Books could be borrowed for a small sum. This was to prevent the destruction of the books which could not be replaced. Lectures were given by anyone who had anything of interest to tell. A large proportion of the men were learning Japanese. A certain Major Wild who acted as interpreter was in charge of this. He had lived for many years in the Far East. Concerts were often held. Cards were by far the most popular game. Bridge and whist tournaments were often held. Football was played a good deal despite the heat. They had even taught the Japanese who soon became too adept at the game and could beat the British. The talk of home was very general and men tended to find those who came from their own part of the country, reminisce and exchange letters and photographs. On the whole, men were too busy and the days passed too quickly for them to feel homesick.

Clothing: This presented a problem as clothing was not replaced, only material suitable for pants or loin cloths. For a year or more, the men were obliged to work without any boots but their feet soon became hardened and they suffered little discomfort. The heat was so great that little clothing was desired. The Officers were necessarily more able to look after their clothes, but nearly all wore either a pair of pants or a loin cloth. Some of the Officers had blankets but few of the men. They were provided with sacks which they tied together and they slept on beds made from split bamboo poles, to which they very soon became accustomed.

Mail: A considerable amount of mail had been received in the Camp. More by Officers than men. This was due to the Japanese who could not be bothered to censor all the mail that arrived, and they make much more of a distinction between Officers and other ranks than we do. Some Officers had received forty or more letters and cards. Most men had been allowed to write five cards home, although most relatives in this country have not received more than three, if as many. Private Ward and Gunner Simpson thought that most of the cards had taken about a year to come to this country.

Deaths: These occurred from time to time when epidemics broke out. Names of casualties have been carefully checked by the War Office from accounts witnessed by the liberated prisoners. At first all deaths were followed by a military funeral for which a Union Flag was used. Eventually this was torn up by the Japanese and no more funerals with military honours were allowed.

> Morale: At all times this was excellent. No man doubted that he would be freed eventually and a general feeling was prevalent that liberation would come in 1945. In any case all men felt able to carry on until that day came. The Japanese tried every kind of propaganda concerning the defeat of the Allies, but no one believed them. While still in Singapore two radio sets were able to be hidden and news was heard but after reaching Thailand this was impossible. However, men were able to get news from civilians who they were able to contact while working. This was a dangerous procedure and punishable if discovered by the guards. A number of men had lived out in the Far East for years and were able to understand the dialect well enough. News of the invasion of France was received only a few days after D-Day. Colonel Lilly arranged for a special service of thanksgiving to be held by the Padre, which greatly incensed the Camp Commandant. Services at all times were held and well attended. Private Ward thought conditions in all the Thailand Camps were much the same.
>
> — — —
>
> I have been requested not to publish the names and addresses of the survivors as they can only give particulars of the general conditions in the Camp. Individual particulars have been taken by the War Office, and will be published in due course.

By way of contrast to the account above, the conditions in the camps were summarized as part of one of the cases during the War Crimes Trials carried out in 1946 as part of the Ishida Case (Singapore Cases: No. 235/963):

1. Accommodation in the camps was generally insufficient. Huts were not weather proof and were made of attap with continuous bamboo sleeping platforms. In monsoon periods, the camps were seas of mud.
2. Food was generally inadequate, more particularly in the interior. What food there was lacked necessary vitamins, was unbalanced and could not maintain health in Europeans.
3. Clothing was rarely issued. The majority of prisoners were forced to go about naked except for a loincloth. Absence of adequate footwear

and trousers caused scratches which, developing into tropical ulcers, often necessitated amputation and sometimes caused death.
4. PoWs were grossly overworked and in some camps, officers were made to work like coolies. A weekly task was set which had to be completed, irrespective of men falling sick or other circumstances. In some cases men were overworked into the night to finish the task.
5. Diseases, particularly deficiency diseases, were rife. Malaria was endemic in most camps and cholera outbreaks occurred. Coolie camps were placed in close proximity to PoW camps so that often the water supply, common to both camps, was fouled before it reached the PoWs.
6. The sick were neglected and, in some cases, brutally treated. Normally only a certain percentage of camp strength was excused from work from sickness. If this number was exceeded on any one day, the surplus sick men nevertheless had to work, despite protests from PoW Doctors. The issue of medical supplies was short. Officially, the issue to PoWs was to be one-third of the scale for Japanese forces, but issues were irregular and often fell short of the scale. Reasonable medical facilities would have avoided many deaths and amputations. It was sometimes possible to buy medical stores in nearby villages and this was occasionally permitted.
7. Latrines were filthy, normally consisting of a shallow open trench with cross slats of bamboo. In heavy rain they overflowed and filth was washed through the camp.
8. PoWs were frequently beaten by Japanese officers, NCOs, Private Soldiers and Korean guards.

Maps

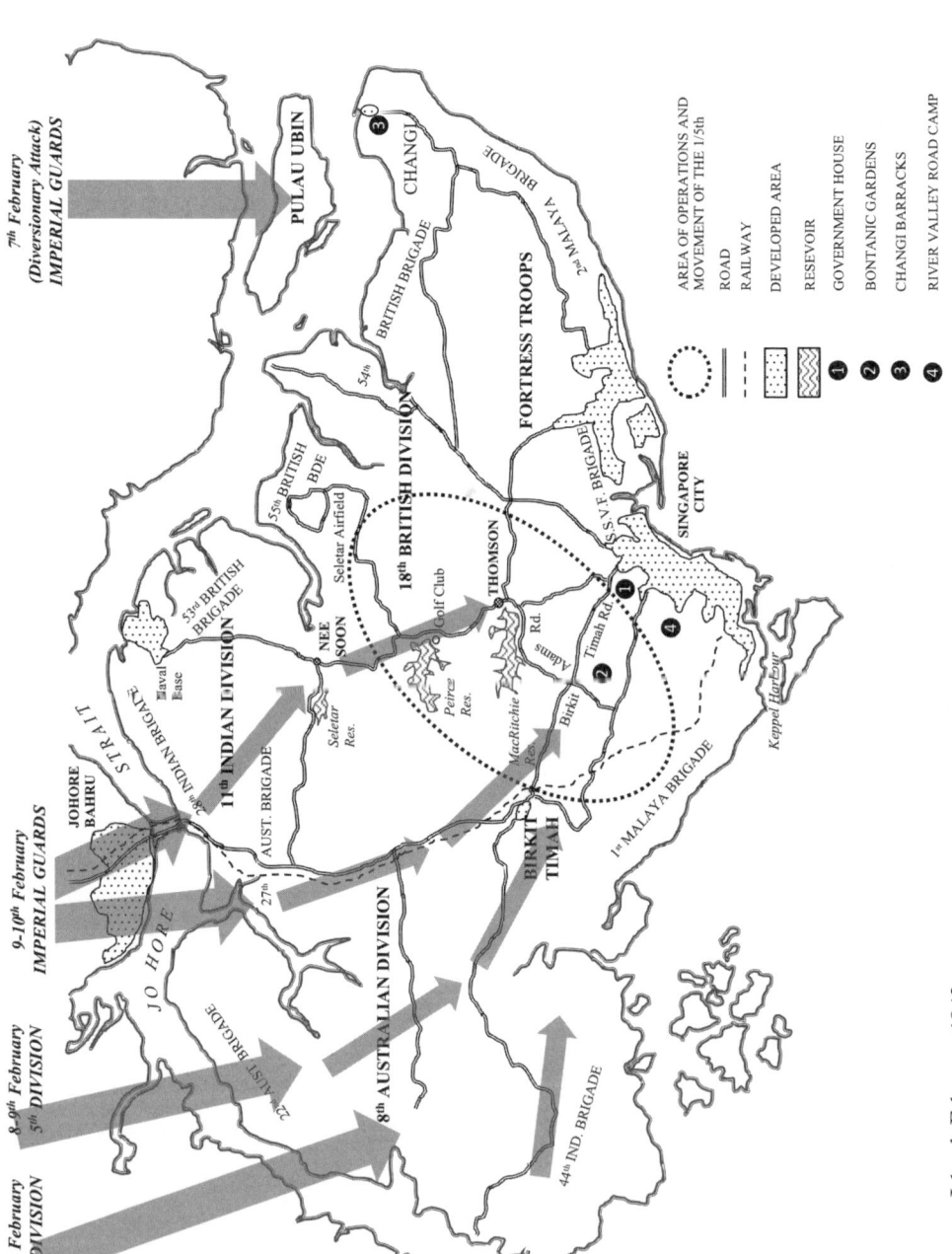

Singapore Island, February 1942.

Sketch map showing the location of the Burma Thai Railway and Eric's route from Singapore.

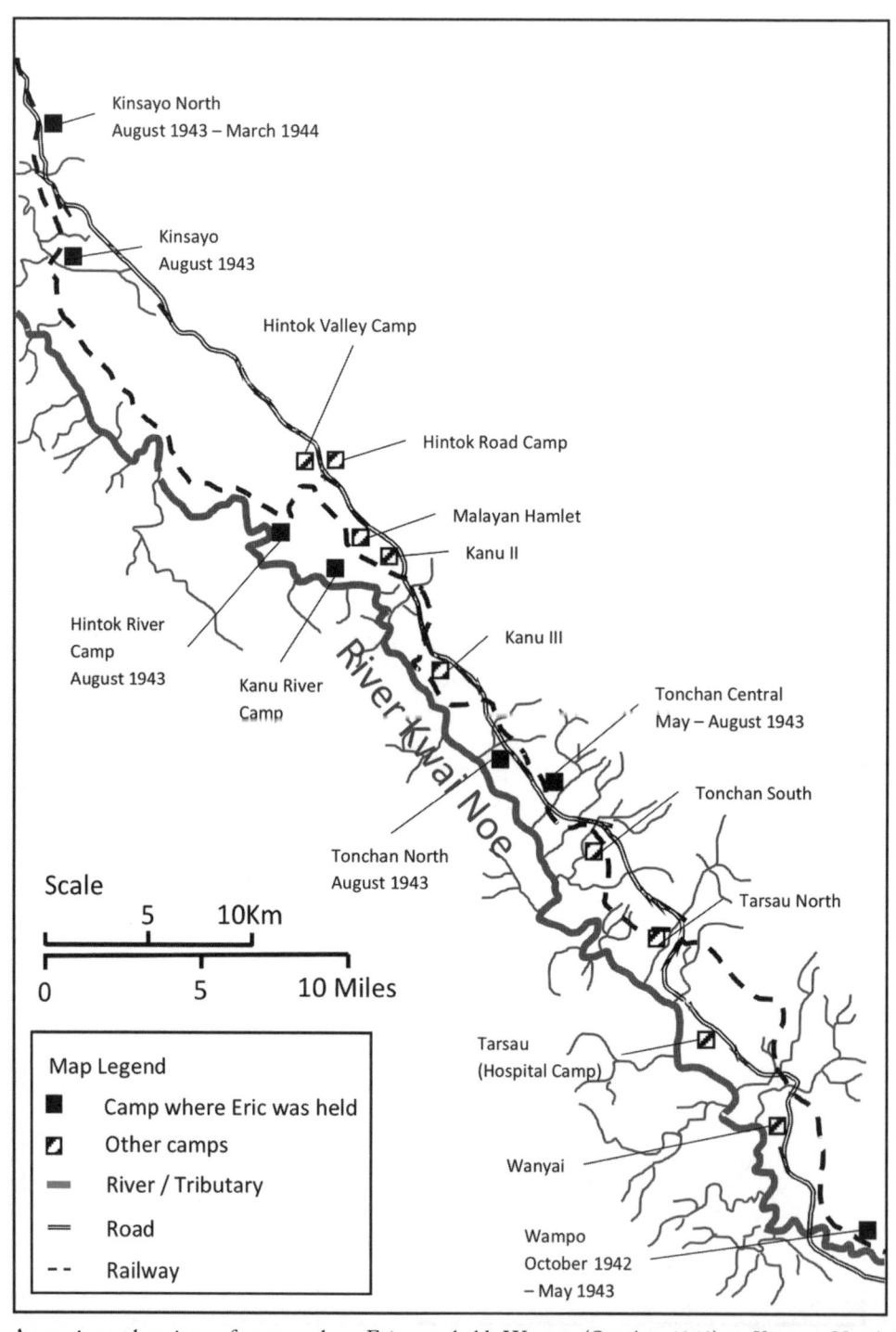

Approximate locations of camps where Eric was held: Wampo (October 1942) to Kinsayo North (March 1944).

Bibliography

Barclay, C.N., *The History of the Sherwood Foresters (Nottinghamshire and Derbyshire Regiment) 1919–1957* (London, 1959)

Churchill, W.S., *The Second World War, Volume 4, The Hinge of Fate* (London, 1952)

Denys Peek, I., *One Fourteenth Of An Elephant* (London, 2005)

Housley, C., *'First In, Last Out', A History of the 1st/5th Territorial Battalion, Sherwood Foresters 1939–1945* (Ilkeston, 1995)

Kelly's Handbook of the Titled, Official and Landed Classes (Kelly's Directories Ltd, 1948)

Pavillard, S.S., *Bamboo Doctor* (London, 1962)

Percival, A.E., *The War in Malaya* (London, 1949)

Russell, E., *The Knights of Bushido* (London, 1958)

Index

3rd Anti-Aircraft Regiment of Artillery, 118
9th Coast Regiment of Artillery, 118
9th Royal Northumberland Fusiliers, 120
18th Division, 16, 39, 41, 49, 51, 63, 67, 78
55th Brigade, 51, 59, 71
80th Anti-Tank Regiment of Artillery, 106
148th Bedfordshire Yeomanry Field Artillery, 106, 117, 132

Adjutant, *see* Coxon
Ali, Wazir, 22
America, SS, *see West Point*, USS
Americanization, 130
American PoWs, 116, 128, 130
Aqaba, 145
Aspdin, Capt. G.S. (75998), 149
Atom Bombs, 126–7
Australian Forces, 35, 39, 60, 115–16, 125, 128–9, 131
Australian PoWs, 60, 115–16, 125, 128–9, 131

B-24 Bombers, 108
Bagnall, Pte J. (4974519), 110–11, 129
Baker, L/Sgt A.A.B. (903873), 132
Barnett, Maj F.W. (41413), 11, 23, 33, 147, 160
Beck, Mrs Jean, 13–14
Beheading, *see* Execution
Birmingham, 10, 23, 29, 44, 48, 63, 66, 74, 99, 150
British Expeditionary Force, 33, 35, 146
British Red Cross, 44, 57, 61, 63, 70–1, 73, 75–7, 97, 98, 100, 113, 131, 156
Brownrigg, Lt J.F. (71179), 34
Burma, 83, 104, 108, 121, 126, 135
Burton Mail, 53, 110
Bushell, Lt H.H. (180398), 106

Cambridgeshire (1st Batt), 102
Cavendish, Lt Col. E.W.S., 149
Chitral, HMS, 89, 140, 144
Cholera, 70, 80, 82, 89, 91–3, 159, 163
Christopher, RSM V.C. (1055584), 118, 126
Churchill, W.C., 40–1, 43, 46, 49, 62
CO, 1/5 Commanding Officer, *see* Lilly
Colombo, 141–4
Cooking, 7, 25, 71, 102, 119, 121, 122, 137, 159
Coxon, Capt A.W. (P/124325), 1, 21, 35–6, 39, 60, 87, 149

'D' Battalion, 79
Degg,
    Jim, 48
    Lilian, 41–2, 45, 48, 52–7, 77, 109, 111, 113
    Ronald, 45, 48, 50, 130, 131, 144
Derby, 1, 14, 54, 147 - 149, 150
Dickenson, Sub Lt P., 72
Dixon, Cpl M.G. (4753908), 67–8, 103
Dorsetshire, HMS, 12
Drayton, 35
Dutch PoWs, 83, 85, 116, 125, 133

Entertainments National Service Association (ENSA), 139
Execution, 106

'F' Battalion, 79
'F' Force, 83
Farrar Park, 60
Federated Malay States Volunteer Force (FMSVF), 80, 103, 116
Formosa, 55

Index

Gibraltar, 145
Gofton-Salmond, Lt Col G.P., 154
Gordon Highlanders (2nd Batt), 62–4

Halfside, Cpl E. (4981054), 152–3
Halifax, Nova Scotia, 5–6, 10, 148
Harris, Lt Col S.W. (44513), 106
Hattari, Lt, 79, 107
Hereford, 150
Hong Kong, 16, 47

Indian Army, 21, 23, 39, 88, 39
Infantry Records, 44–5, 148
Irvine, Lt R.H. (113410), 62
Ishida Case, 162

Japanese Air Force, 33, 37–8
Java, 46
Jews, 69, 70, 83
Jobber, Sgt R.C., 66
Johnson, Alderman T., 149
Jordan, *see* Aqaba

Kachidoki Maru, 110, 153, 156
Kavanagh, Sgt P.R. (7612221), 67
Kelly, Capt, 8
Kempeitai, 131, 150
Kerr, Hon Col J.D., 148–9
Kineton, 139, 147
Koreans, 82, 85, 93, 101–102, 116, 120, 126, 163
Kreiger, Pte A. (4750648), 69–70
Kuala Lumpur, 70

Land Army, 100, 139, 147
Leicester Regiment 1st Batt., 37
Lilly, Lt Col H.H. (2989), 6, 9, 21, 36, 38–40, 60, 67, 70–1, 79, 84, 87, 101, 104, 106, 115, 118–19, 131–4, 148–50, 153–4, 159, 162
Lourenco-Marques, 61

MacDonald, Capt J. (229043), 118
'Madam Butterfly', 116
Massy-Beresford, T.H., 59
Mellor, J.S.P., 75
Mee, Pte C.L. (4982837), 36
Mizutani, Maj. T., 120

Mountbatten, Lady, 131, 133
Mukden, 55, 59

Nanamura, 82
Navy, Army and Air Force Institutes (NAAFI), 146–7
Nicklin, CQMS C.F. (4976632), 87, 149

O'Brien, Pte D., 41–2, 45, 50–2, 95
Orcades, SS, 4–6, 10

Pampanito, USS, 110
Parker, Bette, 17, 47, 48, 53, 56–7, 95, 112–14
Parker, Sgt W.J. (5050759), 7, 17–18, 24, 30, 46–8, 56, 90, 95, 111–13, 134, 137, 143
Pavillard, Capt S.S., 80, 107, 133
Pearl Harbour, 12
Penkridge, 4, 10, 17, 52
Poonah, 21
Port Suez, 144

Queen Alexandra's Imperial Military Nursing Service (QAIMNS), 136

Radio, 1, 7, 117, 127, 162
Rakuyo Maru, 110, 153
Rangoon, 72, 126, 128, 133, 135–6, 138–9, 141, 143, 148, 152
Repatriation of All Prisoners of War and Internees (RAPWI), 136
Redman, Maj, 126–7, 131
Richardson, Capt J. (118168), 93
Roberts, Barbara, 131, 141
Robinson, Maj P.M. (38749), 156–7
Robinson, Mrs Hope, 113, 156–7
Royal Air Force (RAF), 58, 113, 116, 127, 135
Royal Army Chaplaincy Department (RACD), 83
Royal Army Ordnance Corps (RAOC), 67
Royal Army Medical Corps (RAMC), 80, 93, 158–9
Royal Artillery (RA), 79, 106–107, 118, 132, 148, 157
Royal Navy (RN), 12, 31, 72

Saipan, 157
Salvation Army, 7, 11, 18, 30, 48, 112
Sealion, USS, 110
Shirakawa, 55
Simpson, Gnr, 157, 159, 161
Singapore,
   Adams Road, 33–4, 38
   Botanical Gardens, 39
   Bukit-Timah Road, 33, 36, 38
   Changi, 58–60, 71, 83, 120
   Government House, 39, 152
   Seletar, 32
South Africa,
   Cape Town, 12–15, 19, 150
   Del Monico's, 15
   Fisch Hoek, 15
   Port Elizabeth, 12
Southampton, 145
Squires, Bmdr D.G. (916702), 117
Stephens, 2nd Lt M.T.T. (180256), 53, 55
Straits Settlement Royal Naval Volunteer Reserve (SSRNVR), 72
Straits Settlement Volunteer Force (SSVF), 80, 103, 116
Sunda Strait, 31
Suzuki, Capt, 133

Tajiri, 147
Tamils, 92–3
Taylor, Pte C.J.A. (4978065), 42
Thailand,
   Bangkok, 72, 79, 123, 125, 128, 130–1, 135–8, 152–3, 158
   Bangkok University, 128, 135, 138
   Banpong, 70–2, 115, 120
   Kanburi, 71, 120
   Nakom Paton, 88, 90, 121
   Petchburi, 90, 137
   Tarsao, 72, 116, 132
   Wampo, 72, 78, 81–2, 85, 87–8, 103, 150
Thorpe, Capt. N.S. (75410), 53, 55
Three Pagodas, 104
Tiger, The, *see* Watanabe, Sgt
Trinidad, 5, 9–10
Tsumura, Ens, 120
Tukeda, Sgt, 82

Union Flag, 126, 152, 161
United States Navy (USN), 5, 9, 12–13, 15–16, 21, 32, 110

Wanty, Fus L.W. (4272350), 120
War Crimes, 120, 133, 147, 151, 162
Ward, 2nd Lt K.W. (187805), 107
War Graves Commission, 148
Warren, Cpl A.E. (4756233), 132
Watanabe, Sgt, 90–1
Wells, Bmdr, 148
West Point, USS, 6, 10, 12–13, 21, 30–1
White, Cpl G.W.C. (4756254), 28, 32, 38, 59, 67–8, 70–1, 79, 82, 86, 91, 93, 102, 104, 107, 115–17, 126–7, 129, 150, 154–5
Women's Royal Naval Service (WRNS or Wrens), 142–3, 146
Women's Royal Voluntary Service (WRVS), 147
Wood, Cpl W.H. (4976843), 14, 42, 111, 149